Advance Praise for

HOW TO SURVIVE YOUR FRESHMA

"An amazing collection of tips, stories and fun. A tour de ᴜᴏᴜ
A great send-off for every high school senior."

—JEFFREY P. KAHN, PH.D
PROFESSOR, UNIVERSITY OF MINNESOTA, DIRECTOR, CENTER FOR BIOETHICS

"It was nice to know that I'm not alone. Reading this book
lowered my anxiety and prepared me for this year's challenges."

—DANIEL GLUCK
FRESHMAN, UNIVERSITY OF PENNSYLVANIA

"The kind of advice you'd get from an older brother or trusted
friend. Fun, informative and a quick read."

—ELANA BROWNSTEIN
BETH TIFILOH HIGH SCHOOL, BALTIMORE, MARYLAND

"After reading *How to Survive Your Freshman Year*, I now
know what I wish I had known five years ago."

—JAY OWEN
5TH YEAR STUDENT, GEORGIA INSTITUTE OF TECHNOLOGY

"This book is right on the money. I wish I had this before I
started college."

—KATIE LEVITT
SENIOR, GEORGE WASHINGTON UNIVERSITY

"This guide is informative and a great reference for those who
are still in high school, anyone in college or even parents who
might want some insight into their children's lives on campus.
Everyone who might need to know anything and everything
about college life should pick up this guide."

—ANNE KRISTOL
WASHINGTON UNIVERSITY IN ST. LOUIS, FRESHMAN

"This is terrific! What a great collection of advice and experience! This book has everything freshmen need to know to survive— and thrive—in college!"

—DEBRA FELDSTEIN
FORMER EXECUTIVE DIRECTOR, HILLEL, STANFORD UNIVERSITY

"I was nervous about starting college, but now that I've read this book I feel totally confident."

—JON BIRNBREY
SENIOR, RIDGEWOOD HIGH SCHOOL, ATLANTA, GEORGIA

How to
Survive Your
Freshman Year

How to · Survive Your Freshman Year

by **Hundreds** of College Sophomores, Juniors, and Seniors Who Did *

*and some things to avoid, from a few dropouts who didn't

edited by

MARK W. BERNSTEIN AND YADIN KAUFMANN

Hundreds of Heads Books, Inc.

ATLANTA

Copyright © 2004 by Hundreds of Heads Books, Inc., Atlanta, GA

All rights reserved. No portion of this book may be reproduced—mechanically, electronically, or by any other means, including photocopying—without written permission of the publisher.

Trademarks: Hundreds of Heads, Because Hundreds of Heads are Better than One!, and related trade dress are trademarks or registered trademarks of Hundreds of Heads Books, Inc., and may not be used without written permission. All other trademarks are the property of their respective owners. Hundreds of Heads Books, Inc. is not associated with any product or vendor mentioned in this book.

Illustrations © 2004 by Image Club

Library of Congress Control Number: 2004100604

See page 239 for credits and permissions.

Limit of Liability/Disclaimer of Warranty: Every effort has been made to accurately present the views expressed by the interviewees quoted herein. The publisher and editors regret any unintentional inaccuracies or omissions, and do not assume responsibility for the opinions of the respondents. The advice contained herein may not be suitable for your situation (in fact, some of it may be dangerous to your health!). Neither the publisher nor the authors of any of the stories herein shall be liable for any loss of profit or any other commercial damages, including but not limited to special, incidental, consequential, or other damages.

Cover photograph by PictureQuest/Rubberball Productions
Cover and book design by Elizabeth Johnsboen
Interior illustrations by Image Club

HUNDREDS OF HEADS™ books are available at special discounts when purchased in bulk for premiums or institutional or educational use. Excerpts and custom editions can be created for specific uses. For more information, please email info@howisurvived.com or write to:

HUNDREDS OF HEADS BOOKS, INC.
2221 Peachtree Road
Suite D-230
Atlanta, GA 30309

ISBN 0-9746292-0-0

Printed in U.S.A.
10 9 8 7 6 5 4 3 2

CONTENTS

Introduction

When you're about to go through one of life's major challenges or milestones, it's good to get advice from people who have "been there, done that." Why make all the mistakes for yourself? Find out what worked, and what didn't work, from others who have been in similar situations.

This book—the first in the HUNDREDS OF HEADS™ Survival Guide series—grew out of that simple idea.

Other advice books, no matter how smart or expert their authors, are generally limited to the knowledge of only one person. We sought to do something different—to assemble the experiences and wisdom of hundreds of college students who went through freshman year and came out the other side with some insight to share. If two heads are better than one, as the saying goes, then hundreds of them should be even better.

We interviewed students and graduates from big schools, small schools, Ivies, and state universities; Greeks, geeks, and jocks; men and women. What they told us about their college experience— whether satisfied, relieved, or regretful—was remarkably universal. We're sure their views will be useful no matter what school you're attending. You might even be relieved to find that the things you worry about are in fact pretty common concerns, and that people have found lots of ways to deal with them.

As you might expect, we heard many different views—and you'll find often opposite views on the same feature of college life: Are fraternities a good choice or not? Should you live on campus or off? To party or not to party? You'll have to make your own choices, but now you can make those choices armed with the wisdom of all the people featured in the pages ahead.

So read on—chances are, you'll find something in these pages that makes your college experience more enjoyable, rewarding, fun, and successful (as well as a few things that we wouldn't recommend trying).

The real credit for this book goes to all the people whose experiences and collective wisdom make up this guide. Thanks to Casey from Georgetown, Carla from Dominican, Don from Delaware, Hannah from Harvard, Jo from Emory, Pete from Princeton…There are too many of you to thank individually, of course, but you know who you are. Thanks for sharing.

Thanks, too, go to our intrepid "head-hunters" for going out to find so many college students around the country with interesting advice to share: Jamie Allen, Kerry Rodgers, and Beth Turney; as well as Lindsay Brillson, Lisa Powell, Elizabeth Hockstad, David Harris, and Elana Brownstein. A special thanks to our editorial advisor Anne Kostick. Dov Kaufmann was a big help with research.

Mark W. Bernstein
Yadin Kaufmann

Get Ready: What to Take to College

O K, *so college isn't exactly a desert island. Sure, you can get pretty much everything you need at the university store or in town. But here are some not-so-obvious things that you might want to think about bringing to campus with you, as well as suggestions for what to leave at home.*

I HAD A BATTERY-CHARGED, PORTABLE BLENDER. It was super. It cost $50. I was dorm shopping with my dad, and I said, "I need that blender." He was like, "You don't need a portable blender for college." I was like, "No, no, Dad, I need that. Take the comforter out of the cart. I need that." So we got it. And I made everything in it. A blender helps make friends.

—CASEY
GEORGETOWN UNIVERSITY, SENIOR

BRING YOUR BLANKET. MAKE SURE IT'S COMFY.

—CHANA WEINER
BARNARD COLLEGE
SOPHOMORE

Top 10
FRESHMAN
FAVORITES

Sleeping Bag

Guitar

Headphones

Blender

Blankie

Photos

Organizer

Cell Phone

Bible

Toothbrush

BEST GIFT TO ASK FOR FROM YOUR PARENTS: One really great sleeping bag. You'll use it for everything, from spring break in a hotel room with 20 other people, to backpacking across Europe or the U.S.

> —*WENDY W.*
> *UNIVERSITY OF GEORGIA, 1996*

• • • • • • • •

BRING SOME GOOD PAJAMAS. It's uncomfortable sleeping with other people in the same room, but one thing that helps is to have good pajamas that cover most of your body parts. You can lounge around in them without worrying about how you look.

> —*S.G.*
> *COLUMBIA UNIVERSITY, SENIOR*

• • • • • • • •

A NICE TOWEL IS REALLY IMPORTANT. People see you in your towel and you need to look good. Douglas Adams said the towel is the most important piece of equipment in the universe, because you can do so much with it.

> —*TIM JOYCE*
> *GEORGETOWN UNIVERSITY, SENIOR*

• • • • • • • •

BRING LOTS OF BEDDING. Foam "egg crates" are a must. The mattresses at my school are covered in rubber in case you wet the bed or something, so I got a feather bed, and lots of people have foam things. Then you can get a good night's sleep.

> —*EDITH ZIMMERMAN*
> *WESLEYAN UNIVERSITY, SOPHOMORE*

• • • • • • • •

A CASE OF NO-DOZ, Pop-Tarts, and several extra room keys.

> —*S.L.M.*
> *INDIANA UNIVERSITY, 1982*

FOR MY KID IT WOULD LIKELY be an HP calculator or a Bible. For someone else's kid, it would likely be a beer bong or mixed-drink recipe book. And I guess if these kids got together they would have all the bases covered.

> —*S.A.H.*
> *GEORGIA INSTITUTE OF TECHNOLOGY, 1987*

· · · · · · · ·

AN EXCELLENT PAIR OF STUDIO-GRADE headphones for those times when you want to jam but your roommate wants to snooze. You cannot get through college without your music.

> —*MARGOT CARMICHAEL LESTER*
> *UNIVERSITY OF NORTH CAROLINA AT CHAPEL HILL, 1983*

· · · · · · · ·

A Hot Pot. I hated the food at my college, so every other meal I made *Oodles and Noodles.* You can make tea, coffee, soup— anything, really— in a Hot Pot.

> —*ALYSSA*
> *JAMES MADISON UNIVERSITY SOPHOMORE*

❝Communal showers are gross, so bring shower shoes. Everybody wears them, except my roommate. But at least she took showers!❞

> —*SIERRA*
> *CAL POLY SAN LUIS OBISPO, JUNIOR*

· · · · · · · ·

A LAPTOP. If I want to write something at my desk, I just move the laptop aside. Some kids have a big desktop computer and monitor and they have to lie on their bed with something hard to write on.

> —*MATT MONACO*
> *GEORGE WASHINGTON UNIVERSITY, FRESHMAN*

If I could, I'd bring my bed from home.

—*CESAR*
  YALE UNIVERSITY
  FRESHMAN

BRING WARM CLOTHES if you go to school up north. I'm from Miami and I didn't know what a winter coat was. Now I have a couple, and an umbrella.

> —*HILARY TRESS*
> *NEW YORK UNIVERSITY, JUNIOR*

* * * * * * * *

A REALLY NICE CHAIR; something you can move, something that folds up. If there are five or six people in a room, everyone is sitting on the floor. But if you bring in your chair, you can keep it for yourself. Or, if there's that girl, give it up to her and you earn bonus points.

> —*CHRIS PROVENCHER*
> *JAMES MADISON UNIVERSITY, FRESHMAN*

* * * * * * * *

AN ALARM CLOCK. You need it for getting up in the morning, but you also need it for getting up from a nap in the middle of the day.

> —*M.D.*
> *BOSTON COLLEGE, FRESHMAN*

* * * * * * * *

A PALM PILOT or other kind of organizer. It helps.

> —*M.A.A.*
> *GEORGE WASHINGTON UNIVERSITY, SENIOR*

* * * * * * * *

THE BIBLE. I RELIED ON MY FAITH to get me through a lot of hard issues.

> —*A.G.H.*
> *UNIVERSITY OF VIRGINIA, SENIOR*

* * * * * * * *

A TOOTHBRUSH. I wouldn't do well without a toothbrush.

> —*J.P.G.*
> *UNIVERSITY OF PENNSYLVANIA, SOPHOMORE*

A FRISBEE. You can make friends just by going out in the quad and throwing it around. People come by and play.

> —JOSH STAFFORD
> UNIVERSITY OF VIRGINIA, 2002

• • • • • • • •

MY BEER HELMET. And sandals for the shower.

> —JOEL
> PRINCETON UNIVERSITY, 2002

• • • • • • • •

✓ **BRING HEADPHONES.** I have a friend who's into white pop music and she lived with a girl from the Bronx who only liked gangsta rap, and they had this huge friction that basically ruined their roommate relationship.

> —ERIC FRIES
> BOSTON UNIVERSITY, 1997

• • • • • • • •

I FORGOT MY PILLOW. That didn't work out too well. I had to use a rolled-up towel.

> —PATRICK
> UNIVERSITY OF RHODE ISLAND, FRESHMAN

• • • • • • • •

CONTRACEPTIVES: YOU DON'T WANT to make the proverbial mistake that you're stuck with for the rest of your life. There's such a thing as taking a reasonable risk or a stupid risk. That covers sex, drug use, everything.

> —MICHAEL A. FEKULA
> UNIVERSITY OF MARYLAND, 1985

• • • • • • • •

A CELL PHONE. Since you're out so much, if people want to get in touch with you—your parents, your friends from high school, your friends here—it makes it much easier.

> —EAMONN MORAN
> GEORGETOWN UNIVERSITY, JUNIOR

Bring your mom's credit card.

> —J.G.
> GEORGE WASHINGTON UNIVERSITY, SENIOR

MY JOURNAL. IT'S A COMPANION when you don't have one. It sounds cheesy, but I used mine a lot.
>—STEPHANIE
>UNIVERSITY OF PENNSYLVANIA, SENIOR

A MAID.
>—MATT BIGGERSTAFF
>EMORY UNIVERSITY, SENIOR

"Get an alarm clock radio. If you go out late the night before, it's got to be real loud so you actually get up."
>—KEVIN WALSH
>GEORGETOWN UNIVERSITY, SOPHOMORE

A TENNIS BALL. IT'S GREAT TO TOSS AROUND the lounge and in the hallway, and it is a great conversation starter. As you throw the ball around, people come in to toss and the camaraderie begins.
>—DAVE BANVILLE
>AMERICAN UNIVERSITY, 1999

FAKE IDS ARE A GOOD IDEA. My sister said I wouldn't need one until spring semester. That is not true. That is bad advice. If your friends decide to go to a bar, you can go with them. If you don't have an ID, you simply can't go.
>—BAYLESS PARSLEY
>UNIVERSITY OF VIRGINIA, FRESHMAN

GET A KICK-ASS MOUNTAIN BIKE to ride between classes—and an even more kick-ass lock.

—*J.G.*
FLORIDA STATE UNIVERSITY, 1991

FRESHMAN FACTOID

Estimated number of bicycles in use on campus at Stanford University— 15,000.

MY STEREO SYSTEM. I got to have beats. You can drown someone out if you have to, just get into your own little zone.

—*KENTON*
UNIVERSITY OF VIRGINIA, SENIOR

A JOURNAL. It's kind of a manic-depressive time, freshman year. There are really big highs and really big lows. During the lows it helps to write it out.

—*ANONYMOUS*
YALE UNIVERSITY, SOPHOMORE

A BOX FAN OF REASONABLE TORQUE and a bath towel, preferably damp. The fan directed out the dorm window was to create an exhaust vacuum effect while the damp towel, covering the gap at the foot of the door, prevented the escape of any extraneous, ahem, smoke.

—*A.D.*
UNIVERSITY OF NEW HAMPSHIRE

I WOULD DEFINITELY BRING A STEREO. I used to listen to Bach when I was studying. It supposedly enhances your learning. I don't know if it's true.

—*JAKE MALAWAY*
UNIVERSITY OF ILLINOIS, 1995

MY PHOTOS. They kept me grounded.

—*HANNAH SMITH*
HARVARD UNIVERSITY, JUNIOR

ORANGE-FLAVORED GATORADE. More Gatorade is consumed to relieve hangovers than while playing any sport. And stay with orange, because red can stain when it comes back up.

> —*ANONYMOUS*
> *UNIVERSITY OF FLORIDA, 1993*

• • • • • • • •

A BLANKET. Mine is called Blue Fuzzy. Every once in a while you'll find yourself wanting to hide under your blanket.

> —*M.E.G.*
> *UNIVERSITY OF NORTH CAROLINA, 2001*

BRING EXTRA LIGHTING for your dorm room, an air mattress in case a friend comes over, and a fake ID.

> —*JESSICA*
> *BARNARD COLLEGE, JUNIOR*

• • • • • • • •

A NICE WATERPROOF BOOK BAG. If it rains, your books get wet and there's not a lot you can do to fix them. It hurts the sell-back value, too.

> —*B.M.*
> *UNIVERSITY OF MARYLAND, JUNIOR*

• • • • • • • •

Stuffed animals. . . I brought mine!

—*CATHERINE G.*
BARRETT
BRYN MAWR
COLLEGE
SOPHOMORE

A BOOK BY NIETZSCHE. People might think I was intellectual, introspective and maybe a little dark and mysterious. And it would provide some interesting reading.

> —*R.D.W.*
> *UNIVERSITY OF VIRGINIA, 1988*

• • • • • • • •

A MECHANICAL PENCIL WITH A BIG ERASER. If you're like me and you'd rather pay attention in class than do a bunch of reading, a good mechanical pencil is great for taking clean, concise notes.

> —*J.S.*
> *UNIVERSITY OF GEORGIA, 1995*

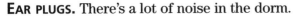
EAR PLUGS. There's a lot of noise in the dorm.

> —*RICK SHILLING*
> *PENN STATE UNIVERSITY, 1998*

• • • • • • • •

A FEW CANDLES, A PACK OF CIGARETTES, and some good poetry.

> —*ANONYMOUS*
> *CALVIN COLLEGE, 2000*

• • • • • • • •

UNDERWEAR.

> —*WALTER*
> *UNIVERSITY OF MARYLAND-COLLEGE PARK, SOPHOMORE*

• • • • • • • •

A GEORGE FOREMAN GRILL. Those grills are so fast and easy, and everything is pretty good, from steak to grilled cheese. No college kid should be without one.

> —*JEFF*
> *BOWLING GREEN STATE UNIVERSITY, 2001*

• • • • • • • •

✔ **MY LAPTOP AND MY FAVORITE MOVIE.**
While I used my laptop for almost all my work, it was especially important to me for sending and receiving instant messages with my friends. And whenever I had a bad day, I would pop my favorite movie in the VCR and begin to feel better within minutes. I must have watched *When Harry Met Sally* 100 times during my freshman year. It was an emotional lifesaver.

> —*DANIELLE FRIEDMAN*
> *DUKE UNIVERSITY, SENIOR*

• • • • • • • •

BRING AN UMBRELLA. Yes, it rains at college, too.

> —*PHIL*
> *UNIVERSITY OF VIRGINIA, SENIOR*

Bring your wallet and a lot of money.

—*COLIN O'CONNOR*
GEORGETOWN UNIVERSITY, JUNIOR

WHAT *NOT* TO BRING

If I could go back and not buy a computer, that's what I'd do. And I've never used IM, and I get by. Here's how it works: Because I don't have a computer in my room, I'm never in my room. Since I'm never in my room, I'm always outside in the quad. Since I'm always in the quad, I see my friends. Since I'm always seeing my friends out here, I don't need to see them on IM. The reason you need IM is because you're always in your room with your computer. It creates its own problem and solves its own problem. Get rid of the computer and you won't need IM. And you can spend that $1,500 on beer and food and spring break trips.

    —RICH MURPHY
     GEORGETOWN UNIVERSITY, JUNIOR

- - - - - - - - -

I just didn't know what to bring, so I kept packing every little thing I might need or want to have with me. I would have brought my bathroom and bed, too! When I got to school I had no place to put anything. I ended up bringing back as much stuff as I could each time I went home. After break, I came back up with only the things I really needed.

    —ILANA COOPERSMITH
     RUTGERS UNIVERSITY, 2002

- - - - - - - - -

Do not download AOL Instant Messenger. That will be the end of you. That is the greatest procrastination tool known to man. I wish I had never discovered that stupid thing. I hate it. It's a leash. People keep you on a leash with that.

    —MIKE PARKER
     GEORGETOWN UNIVERSITY, SOPHOMORE

I came here with my dad's station wagon and a minivan filled with my stuff. About a week ago, my parents came back and we packed the station wagon back up and sent stuff back home. It was too much. I brought my notes from my classes in high school. I brought my books from home. I didn't even want to look at a book or notes unless it was from a current class.

—*H.D.BALLARD*
UNIVERSITY OF VIRGINIA, FRESHMAN

• • • • • • • •

Don't be the only person in your dorm with a car, and if you are, don't let other people borrow it. If you do, there will be trouble.

—*HANNAH*
EMORY UNIVERSITY, JUNIOR

• • • • • • • •

You can get by without a computer and a printer: It's not that difficult. I don't have a cell phone, and I've never had one. You don't really need books because you can go to the library and get the books. You don't need anything, really. You can sleep on someone's floor. You can borrow people's shampoo or soap. You could borrow someone's deodorant. You don't really need anything.

—*MARTIN*
GEORGETOWN UNIVERSITY, SOPHOMORE

• • • • • • • •

There's not enough space to keep your stuff, so don't bring a lot of stuff.

—*MARINNA FADOR*
BOSTON COLLEGE, FRESHMAN

A BIBLE IS AUTOMATIC. It's something aesthetic you can bring from home. If you want to look at it every day, you can. I remember, after September 11, everyone was in the middle of my hall, praying. So it always helps.

—*JERI D. HILT*
HOWARD UNIVERSITY, SENIOR

• • • • • • • •

A GUITAR. IT'S SOMETHING THAT RELAXES ME, and it helps socially. You can always pull out your guitar and play on the lawn or wherever, and other people will come up and talk.

—*LEAH PRICE*
GEORGETOWN UNIVERSITY, SOPHOMORE

• • • • • • • •

I WOULD BRING MY PILLOW—it smells like my sleep.

—*ANONYMOUS*
UNIVERSITY OF RHODE ISLAND, SOPHOMORE

2 Get Set: Leaving Home

No matter where you come from, and no matter where you're going, taking that step from high school to college will be a major change in your life. Although there's no way around it, you'll get through it.

LEAVING FAMILY IS A BIG ADJUSTMENT. I got lonely my first year and my parents were pretty strict about keeping me at school until I got over it. It was very hard but I grew from it. When I joined the football team, they came up for games, which was great. But the way I fought it mostly was by keeping busy; that's the best way. It's still hard.

—RYAN SMITH
CARNEGIE MELLON UNIVERSITY, JUNIOR

SAY GOODBYE, KISS THEM, AND MAKE THEM DRIVE AWAY QUICKLY.

—C.H.
UNIVERSITY OF VIRGINIA, FRESHMAN

Getting
dropped off
was like noth-
ing else. My
parents were
crying, so I
felt pretty
awkward. I
wasn't crying,
but I was
moved, for
lack of a bet-
ter word.

—*R.J.*
UNIVERSITY OF
DELAWARE
SOPHOMORE

I HAD A REALLY GOOD TIME AFTER I committed myself. I think it's all a matter of making the decision that you want to be there and you want to be doing what you're doing. People spent a lot of time choosing the college they want to go to. It makes a big difference if you're excited about where you end up.

> —*ANNE*
> *GEORGE WASHINGTON UNIVERSITY, SENIOR*

• • • • • • • •

I AM REALLY ATTACHED TO MY FAMILY and was hor-rified to leave them. My mom cried, and my dad had tears in his eyes and he never cries, and my little brother, who's 10, was affected by my par-ents. But I coped with it better than I thought. I thought I was going to be bawling, but I was a lot less homesick. I thought I would've been the most homesick person on this campus, but it wasn't that bad. You just have to make it quick.

> —*C.H.*
> *UNIVERSITY OF VIRGINIA, FRESHMAN*

• • • • • • • •

BEFORE COLLEGE, I NEVER WAS AWAY from my fam-ily a lot and didn't sleep out of the house a lot. So, it was very weird to be away from my family. To cope with that, I joined a group and called home a lot. Eventually, I felt better.

> —*ANONYMOUS*
> *UNIVERSITY OF RHODE ISLAND, SOPHOMORE*

• • • • • • • •

I WENT THROUGH A LOT OF CHANGES my freshman year. I came from a very small town in Connecticut. Everybody was white, everybody was middle class to upper middle class. You come to Maryland and all of a sudden you're in a very diverse community that looks like the rest of the world. So you have to be open-minded.

> —*MICHAEL A. FEKULA*
> *UNIVERSITY OF MARYLAND, 1985*

I WENT TO COLLEGE IN THE SAME AREA I grew up in. I didn't think it would be that great; I'd have my mom breathing down my neck all the time. But actually it's really nice. I forgot to bring some stuff and I just went home and got it. And I can go home anytime and take a bath.

> —*LUCY LINDSEY*
> *HARVARD UNIVERSITY, FRESHMAN*

" "I was sadder to leave my friends than my parents. I'll see my parents again and they won't change. But leaving all my high school friends . . . everyone's going to be different, because they all went to different schools."

> —*BAYLESS PARSLEY*
> *UNIVERSITY OF VIRGINIA, FRESHMAN*

MY PARENTS DROVE 12 HOURS to bring me to school. My mom cried after they dropped me off, but not in front of me. I'm actually kind of homesick right now. I look for good airfares and fly home when I can.

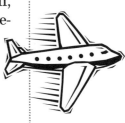

> —*LAUREN WEBSTER*
> *BARNARD COLLEGE, JUNIOR*

THE BIGGEST CULTURE SHOCK WAS GETTING USED to the language. I'm Israeli: Because of the language difficulties, I think I'm a different person because everything I say, I have to think twice before I say it because it sounds different in English.

—*T.G.*
BOSTON UNIVERSITY, SOPHOMORE

. . . .

"It's better going to a college far, far away, because when you need something done, or you miss your family, you have to stick through it. When you're at a college close by, it's hard because your parents still think you're in high school and want to see you every day."

—*KATIE HOLDEN*
RUTGERS UNIVERSITY, FRESHMAN

. . . .

A LOT OF WHAT COLLEGE IS ABOUT IS GETTING PAST a lot of preconceived notions. Be prepared for change.

—*MICHAEL A. FEKULA*
UNIVERSITY OF MARYLAND, 1985

I HAD A HARD TIME ADJUSTING TO COLLEGE LIFE. It was the first time I was permanently away from my family. It was a shock. It wasn't like summer camp, when you know you'll be going back home. If you get sick at college, you're on your own; you can't call Mom and get some soup. You've got to go to the drug- store and get medicine; you can't just go to the medicine cabinet. You can go down to student health, but you have to make your own appointment and you have to walk down there and if it's winter, then it's cold. You have to take care of it yourself.

> —*JESSICA*
> *UNIVERSITY OF PENNSYLVANIA, JUNIOR*

. . . .

YOU DON'T HAVE TO MAKE ANY CHOICES your freshman year. You just need to stay in school, make it to the next year. Every deci- sion you make freshman year can be undone. Keep everything wide open.

> —*JUAN GONZALEZ*
> *CLEMSON UNIVERSITY, 1988*

. . . .

I WAS EXPECTING MY MOM to be sadder. She was like, "All right, see ya." I was like, "Is that it? That's all I get?" But I was the third one to get dropped off. They were sad the first time.

> —*M.A.S.*
> *UNIVERSITY OF VIRGINIA, 1999*

. . . .

MY FAMILY LIVES IN OMAN, so it was hard for my mom: when she dropped me off, she knew I wouldn't be back for Thanksgiving. It's hard to leave your parents: You're used to the family environment so much more.

> —*NATASHA PIRZADA*
> *GEORGETOWN UNIVERSITY, SOPHOMORE*

I THOUGHT I WAS GOING TO HATE COLLEGE. My parents dropped me off my first day and were leaving me there, and I looked at them and said, "I don't think this is going to work out. Can I just come back to the hotel with you guys?" They were just like, "Nope, sorry." My mom got in the car and started crying. And my dad was like, "She'll figure it out." I stayed and I ended up having a great time in school.

—*J. Devereux*
Georgetown University, 2002

• • • • • • • •

My PARENTS WERE REALLY UPSET when they dropped me off. I was upset, for sure, but I was ready to get out of there.

—*Kristin Thomas*
James Madison University, Junior

Go: Starting Out

Y*ou're about to embark on some of the best four (or five, or six) years of your life—but it probably won't seem that way from your first few days on campus. No wonder you're feeling a little queasy underneath the excitement. Here's some battle-tested advice for making the most of those orientation days and getting your college career off to a good start.*

WHEN I WAS A SENIOR IN HIGH SCHOOL, I participated in the Upward Bound program, which allows high school students to experience college life for a week. I lived in the dorms, sat in on classes, met professors, and ate in the cafeteria. It made my transition to freshman year very smooth.

—CARLA BONILLA
DOMINICAN UNIVERSITY, FRESHMAN

SMILE. IT HELPS.
—CASEY
GEORGETOWN UNIVERSITY, SENIOR

COLLEGE GIRL REINVENTED

People always say you can reinvent yourself when you go to college. This is only partially true. You are who you are when you get to college—it's what you do with yourself that changes when you get to college.

I thought for sure I would spend my first semester locked in my room, leaving only under the severest conditions—class, food and bathroom breaks. One problem: that would never work. Upon arriving at school I had people constantly knocking on my door, to ask for a hand in moving furniture, or just to say hi. After conquering my first day I was ready to take on the next, and then I realized: I can actually do this.

The second night of college I walked up to a group of people playing a game of Ultimate Frisbee and asked if I could join in. What? I couldn't even *throw* a Frisbee, let alone play Ultimate Frisbee! What was I thinking? I had a complete brain fart on my initial plan of keeping to myself and hoping for the best. I just threw out all my inhibitions, crossed my fingers and went with it. That night I ended up meeting some of my closest friends to this day, or at least the people who would introduce me to my social network.

—KAREN MICHELLE
STATE UNIVERSITY OF NEW YORK AT NEW PALTZ, SOPHOMORE

DON'T TRY TO FIND A GROUP OF FRIENDS. First, meet as many people as possible and wait until later to find your group.

—*JENNIFER A. SICKLICK*
GEORGE WASHINGTON UNIVERSITY, FRESHMAN

• • • • • • • •

THE FIRST DAY, MOST FRESHMEN HAD NO IDEA how to get from their dorm rooms to their classes. They were pitifully obvious, standing around the bus stops, trying to read the bus route maps inconspicuously. The worst cases were the poor geeks tracing the routes with their fingers. So arrive on campus early. The week before classes start, just get on the main bus route near your dorm. Ride the entire route—learn where it goes. Then do the same for each of the other routes. That way, when classes start you won't be late, lost, or an obvious neophyte.

—*TONYA SMITH*
UNIVERSITY OF GEORGIA, 1987

• • • • • • • •

WHEN YOU MOVE INTO YOUR NEW ROOM, choose the bed where people will see you when the door is open. While you are moving in, people will walk by and see you setting up your room and will stop and say hi.

—*B.K.*
CORNELL UNIVERSITY, 1996

• • • • • • • •

I SKIPPED ALL THE ORIENTATIONS. My sister told me I didn't have to go to them if I didn't want to. So I took that as, "go to the bar instead." But that's not the best advice. That way, all you meet are bar people. I never knew the other three-quarters of our class that didn't go to bars.

—*CASEY*
GEORGETOWN UNIVERSITY, SENIOR

Keep your Social Security number handy for the first several days.

—*BRIAN TURNER*
UNIVERSITY OF GEORGIA, 1996

Don't be afraid to go up to people and introduce yourself.

—MANI
UNIVERSITY OF
MARYLAND
FRESHMAN

☆ **THE CRUCIAL PART OF MY FRESHMAN YEAR** was the first two weeks. The first two weeks you realize who are going to be your best friends throughout the entire year. Your first two weeks you walk around and you go into everybody's room and you see what they're all about—the posters they're putting up and what music they're listening to—and you can pretty much tell from that if you're going to get along with them.

—MIKE ODA
SANTA CLARA UNIVERSITY, SOPHOMORE

• • • • • • • •

THE FIRST FEW WEEKS, freshmen move around in packs. Try to make friends with some upperclassmen. You're more likely to get into parties without a herd of freshmen around you.

—KEVIN WALSH
GEORGETOWN UNIVERSITY, SOPHOMORE

• • • • • • • •

AT FIRST, I WAS LIKE, "DO I REALLY HAVE TO live here for a year?" It was so not like home: There was nothing on the walls. I felt like I was on vacation for the first week of school. I had nothing to do. But then classes started and I had a lot to do.

—AMY HOFFBERG
UNIVERSITY OF DELAWARE, FRESHMAN

• • • • • • • •

I REMEMBER WALKING INTO my first lecture hall and saying, "Wow!" There were 700 people in one room and I was shocked. Then the kid behind me whispered, "Aww, freshman." It only took one class for me to get used to the atmosphere. It wasn't so bad!

—ORLY COBLENS
UNIVERSITY OF MICHIGAN, FRESHMAN

IT WAS HARD TO LEAVE MY PARENTS. I was excited but I was also crying and sad. There's nothing you can do: you just suck it up. Don't spend time alone. Your first week you want to spend time with other kids. Calling home is not all it's cracked up to be: you'll just get more depressed. Once you're at school, just be at school.

—*BETHANY*
JAMES MADISON UNIVERSITY, SENIOR

• • • • • • • •

COLLEGE WAS AT FIRST A HORRIFIC and strange experience for me because the world was larger than I thought it was. But everyone has to start somewhere. Don't feel scared or inferior, because everyone around you had to start out where you are!

—*K. HARMA*
WESTERN WASHINGTON UNIVERSITY, 2001

• • • • • • • •

DON'T TRAVEL IN HERDS THE FIRST WEEK. For example, when attending the obligatory frat parties and keggers, don't travel to and from with your entire dorm. Everyone will know you are a freshman. Choose a couple of people to go with and try to blend in.

—*ANONYMOUS*

BEFORE YOU START, TALK TO A CURRENT STUDENT or recent alumni and ask them for advice. It may be worthless, but it may help you avoid some pitfalls.

—*ANONYMOUS*
UNION COLLEGE

The teachers are going to try to scare you the first week or two and you'll feel overwhelmed. But just keep on track.

—*GREG*
JAMES MADISON UNIVERSITY, JUNIOR

Don't be too shy to ask for help. A lot of people are confused, but if you're lost together, there's more chance of getting it right.

—Alfie Williams
Georgia Institute
of Technology
Sophomore

THE LIVING IS COMPLETELY DIFFERENT. At home, my parents took care of everything. It's a big adjustment: doing laundry, cleaning dishes, going out and getting food. I get back to school from a vacation and I forget—I'm kind of expecting my friends to be making food.

> *—Matt Monaco*
> *George Washington University, Freshman*

• • • • • • • •

WHEN MY PARENTS DROPPED ME OFF, it wasn't that bad. They dropped me off, I sat in my room for a little bit, then I opened my door and started talking with my neighbors. That's how it happens.

> *—Dan Jones*
> *University of Delaware, Senior*

• • • • • • • •

ONE OF THE BIGGEST CHALLENGES I've encountered is finding time to eat at the dining hall. The first week I was here, I hardly ate at all because I didn't know when to go and didn't have enough people to go with. I hate going there alone. You walk in and you don't know which table to sit at. You can sit with anyone and they'll probably be nice about it. But you feel like you have to go with someone, just for security.

> *—C.H.*
> *University of Virginia, Freshman*

• • • • • • • •

IT WAS PRETTY HECTIC THE FIRST DAY. You had to unload your stuff real quick and put it in your room and say goodbye to your parents. My parents were pretty sad. They were like, "I guess you're on your own now." Part of me wanted to get away, and part of me didn't.

> *—Anonymous*
> *University of Maryland, Freshman*

DON'T EVEN THINK ABOUT IT

DO NOT show up with mono and bronchitis. When you arrive at school all you'll want to do is smoke tons of dope and kiss the ladies, both of which are contraindicated treatments for your affliction.

DO NOT think that the type of mono and bronchitis you have won't be contracted by the young lady with whom you spend your first few days at school kissing and smoking dope.

DO NOT think that it's perfectly acceptable to kiss the roommate of the young lady you've been kissing, just because it's late and you and the roommate have been drinking in a dark room alone, smoking tons of dope, and her breasts seem oh so lovely.

DO NOT think that either one of the roommates will accept your proposals to go on kissing both of them behind the back of the other roommate.

DO NOT think that the roommates will not share stories and commiserate and call you a philandering bastard behind your back, especially once they figure out they both have mono.

DO NOT think that it's just fine to smoke even a tiny bit of dope at this point.

And when you're in the hospital with double viral pneumonia for two weeks, **DO NOT** expect that either of the roommates will come visit you.

—*LEE KLEIN*
 OBERLIN UNIVERSITY, 1994

STARTING OUT, EVERYBODY IS BASICALLY LOST. You might look around and think you're the only one who is lost. But everyone is going through the same thing.

—*JOHNNY*
GEORGETOWN UNIVERSITY, JUNIOR

• • • • • • • •

TRY TO BE AS OUTGOING AS YOU CAN. All the people that I'm friends with now I met the first two or three weeks. You end up being closest with the people that you meet early on—because you're all in the same situation, going through the same thing. You're all in a new school, no one knows anyone.

—*CHIP JONES*
HAMILTON COLLEGE, JUNIOR

• • • • • • • •

"**Find a campus map. The weekend before classes begin, figure out where all your classes are. You'll feel much more at ease on the first day.**"

—*WENDY W.*
UNIVERSITY OF GEORGIA, 1996

• • • • • • • •

I JUST HAVE TO GO UP TO PEOPLE I DON'T KNOW and try to make friends. It's a lot different from high school, where everyone knows you, and you're friends with everybody.

—*KEVIN BUSHEY*
GEORGIA STATE UNIVERSITY, FRESHMAN

THINGS WON'T BE PERFECT AT THE BEGINNING.
You're going to have a couple of rough months
when you're trying to find your niche and remember why on earth you came to college. But give
yourself time to integrate, to decide how you
want to spend your time, who you want to spend
your time with, and what kind of people will
complement those objectives. You can drive yourself crazy trying to do everything with all sorts of
people or you can try to figure out what makes
you happy and who you're comfortable with. But
that won't happen immediately. It takes at least a
year, maybe a little longer.

—*ANONYMOUS*
UNIVERSITY OF VIRGINIA, SENIOR

• • • • • • • •

JUST GIVE IT TIME. At first, I would call or
IM some of my old buddies from high
school, talking with old friends. It was good to
have some close friends as a sounding board for
the things I was going through.

—*WONNIE RYU*
EMORY UNIVERSITY, SENIOR

• • • • • • • •

CAN YOU HANDLE THIS?

At Knox College, they figure your body is nice and
relaxed after a summer off. So the college invented a little tradition known as the Pump Handle: Everyone forms
a greeting line, and the president of the college shakes
hands with each of the hundreds of students, faculty and
staff. No problem, right? Except that when he's done,
every last one of those hundreds of students, faculty and
staff has to shake hands with every other person, too.

I MADE MOST OF MY FRIENDS IN THE BEGINNING.
You start off hanging out in a big group and then
you realize whom you relate to and those are the
people you spend your time with.

> —*ANDREW KARELITZ*
> *UNIVERSITY OF PENNSYLVANIA, FRESHMAN*

• • • • • • • •

THE FIRST FEW MONTHS WERE EASIER than I
thought they would be. But everyone I knew hit a
patch right before they went home, after they'd
been here for a couple of months. It was easy to
come here, but after a couple of months you start
to miss the security of home. Especially when the
tests start.

> —*D.F.*
> *NEW YORK UNIVERSITY, SENIOR*

On Campus or Off: Where to Live

Y*our housing situation is one of the most important choices you'll make, and chances are you'll have to make it even before you get to college. Some schools offer so many options it's hard to know what to do, but here's what some survivors of on-campus and off-campus living have to say.*

MAKE SURE THAT YOU LIVE IN AN ON-CAMPUS dorm your freshman year. If you live off campus, you miss out on so much of the experience of being a freshman. I am twelve years removed from my college graduation and at my wedding, three out of the five groomsmen were guys I met my freshman year in the dorms. I am certain that they will be lifelong friends; we know too many stories about each other to let any one of us get away.

—*ANONYMOUS*
UNIVERSITY OF FLORIDA, 1990

DORM LIFE IS AN ESSENTIAL EXPERIENCE.
—*MELISSA K. BYRNES*
AMHERST COLLEGE
2000

It's much more fun living with other people than living by yourself.

—*Matt Lackner*
Princeton
University
2002

MY FRESHMAN YEAR WAS THE BEST YEAR of my life. Within two days of arriving I had made some of the best friends I've ever had. I lived in a freshman dorm, which I recommend very highly. Everyone is going through the same things you are, and they're all looking to make friends, so it makes for a tight-knit community. In the mixed dorms there are a lot of people who already have their friends, so they just aren't as outgoing.

> —*T.P.*
> *Stanford University, Senior*

LIVE IN THE DORMS WITH FRESHMEN and small ratty rooms. It doesn't sound right, I know, but it's what I wish I had done. My school had a variety of dorms that ran from old, predominantly freshman dorms with tiny, two-person rooms, to newly renovated, upper-classman dorms that were like six-person apartments. I chose the middle of the road; a mostly upperclassman dorm with large rooms. Big mistake. These types of dorms aren't conducive to meeting lots of people, which is what freshman year is all about.

Through a classmate in one of the older dorms with tiny rooms, I discovered a social wonderland. Everyone in the building was a freshman, everyone kept their doors open, and everyone wandered around meeting and greeting. There was pretty much a family or little town atmosphere, everyone hung out and did lots of stuff together. This is what the freshman experience was supposed to be.

> —*Jeff*
> *Bowling Green State University, 2001*

I LIVE OFF CAMPUS. It's great—I'm much more focused on my work, because when I come home, I'm able to concentrate on my studies. The dorms are great, but there are way too many distractions, people always dropping by your room.

—*TOM CHRISTENSEN*
DOMINICAN UNIVERSITY, SENIOR

• • • • • • • •

I'M AN ONLY CHILD and I lived with three girls in one big room. It was a pretty big adjustment the first semester. I remember being kind of miserable. You don't get much sleep and there's a lot of work to do. But you get through it.

—*ANNE*
GEORGE WASHINGTON UNIVERSITY, SENIOR

66 Don't live in the dorms. There's too much going on, everybody's always messing around. I suggest living off campus the first year, just because you'll get a lot more done. 99

—*BRYAN FITZGERALD*
GEORGIA INSTITUTE OF TECHNOLOGY, JUNIOR

• • • • • • • •

TRY TO GET PLACED IN THE FRESHMAN DORMS. Even though the long elevator wait and community bathrooms seem horrible—and they are—you won't meet anyone if you live in the smaller, nicer dorms.

—*ASHLEY LEAVELL*
BOSTON UNIVERSITY, SENIOR

Dorms are a good place if you can deal with living in a box with another person.

—K.M.
NORTHWESTERN UNIVERSITY, 2001

I LIVED IN DORMS FOR THE FIRST TWO YEARS. I lived in an all-girl dorm, and for the first two weeks, everyone was happy. But then we all started getting our periods at the same time, and everyone became bitchy all together. It was terrible. And the dorm was filthy. You'd think an all-girl dorm would be clean, but girls are definitely dirtier than guys. Our bathroom was disgusting. And the end of the year was ridiculous—we had garbage cans spilling into the hallways. Living off campus now is like a slice of heaven.

—SUSAN LIPPERT
EMORY UNIVERSITY, JUNIOR

• • • • • • • •

I LIVED OFF CAMPUS. It was a hard transition. I had to take the bus every day to classes and I was away from the social life on campus. Taking the bus was a pain in the ass; I had to get up an hour before class in the morning. And going to parties on campus was a pain, because buses didn't run that late at night.

—ALEC
BOSTON COLLEGE, JUNIOR

• • • • • • • •

LIVING AT HOME AND GOING TO SCHOOL isn't bad at all. It's fine with me, I mean, college rooms are pretty small, and I wake up early enough to beat the traffic.

—ERIC CABRERA
GEORGIA STATE UNIVERSITY, FRESHMAN

• • • • • • • •

I LIVED IN A CO-OP MY FIRST YEAR, so I wasn't pampered by the dorms. It's chaos 100 percent of the time, but it's worth it. It's about self-sufficiency. We don't go to the army after high school, like they do in Israel. Here we go to college, so here is where we need to learn independence, develop a thick skin, and learn how to balance life.

—KATE LEFKOWITZ
UNIVERSITY OF CALIFORNIA AT BERKELEY, JUNIOR

OFF-CAMPUS FOLLIES

I thought living in a dorm would be stifling and stupid. Instead, I got an apartment next to campus with three other roommates. Now *that* was stupid. Friends from the dorms—and their friends—considered our place Party Central, since they had no other place to go and were too young to get into bars. There was a parade of people in and out of the place almost every night—not to mention an abundance of alcohol and drugs. The police came four different times, warning us to quiet down. Regulars included the entire trumpet section of the marching band, a five-piece rock band of bare-chested guys, a torch-juggling   pharmacy student and a cross-dresser named Phil. The apartment was trashed and I was always afraid of getting in big legal trouble. I tried to kick everyone out, but my roommates refused to back me up. At the end of the year, I packed up my stuff and moved into the dorms.

—W.
UNIVERSITY OF GEORGIA, 1996

IF YOUR PARENTS LIVE LOCALLY, resist the temptation and the savings to live at home. I lived at home and it was a big mistake. There are two reasons. First is the commute: I missed an important quiz one day because I missed my bus, and it really cost me. It is a hassle to schlep back and forth. The second reason is the bonding: Most kids make their best friendships with kids who live in or around their dorm or frat. I missed that bonding and never made it up.

> NAYEMA
> CARNEGIE MELLON UNIVERSITY, SOPHOMORE

* * * * * * * *

LIVE ON CAMPUS. Even if you're not required to do it, do it anyway. It makes for a better experience. If you're from far away, it gives you a family environment.

> —LINDSEY FISCHER
> EMORY UNIVERSITY, SENIOR

* * * * * * * *

IF YOU HAVE A CHOICE not to live in the dorms, never live in the dorms. If you have to work to pay for an apartment, work to pay for the apartment. The dorms are not worth the time.

> —ROBIN JALEEL
> EMORY UNIVERSITY, 2002

* * * * * * * *

DON'T PICK COED DORMS. The guys on our floor were doing illegal drugs and I didn't like that. I didn't get along with them, and I didn't get to bond with other girls. If I could do it over I would choose an all-girl dorm; I think I would make more friends that way.

> —TYLER MARIE FREEBERG
> UNIVERISTY OF CALIFORNIA AT SANTA BARBARA, JUNIOR

LIVE IN A DORM and get the freshman experience. You don't have the amenities that you have in an apartment, but you have the experience; sharing the hall, sharing space with roommates.

> —*JESSICA*
> *UNIVERSITY OF PENNSYLVANIA, JUNIOR*

• • • • • • • •

WE HAD MICE. We had a sewer pipe break in our building, and all these little mice were running around. So we set traps. Our hall worked together to catch them; it was teamwork.

> —*LAUREN WEBSTER*
> *BARNARD COLLEGE, JUNIOR*

• • • • • • • •

DORM ROOMS AREN'T BAD—I mean, you just need to know how to organize your stuff. I don't have any problems, really. All my roommates get along, and there's no conflict. You know how guys are—we just go with the flow, there's nothing we need to agree on.

> —*JESSE SAFO*
> *GEORGIA STATE UNIVERSITY, FRESHMAN*

• • • • • • • •

UNUSUAL HOUSING OPTIONS

• Schiller International University (Florida) has university-owned and -operated hotels
• Springfield College (Massachusetts) has an 81-acre "campground and outdoor adventure area"
• Southern Vermont College boasts a 27-room Edwardian mansion
• Taylor University (Indiana) has a "NASA-approved clean room" for the neat freaks

LEARNING TO LIVE WITH PEOPLE—even people you don't like—is an important skill to have.

—*MELISSA K. BYRNES*
AMHERST COLLEGE, 2000

• • • • • • • •

I MADE MY CORE GROUP OF FRIENDS by living in the dorm freshman year.

Relationships are based more on physical proximity than anything else, so most of your friends are probably going to come from your dorm.

—*CAITLIN BERBERICH*
UNIVERSITY OF GEORGIA, 2001

Dorms: The Good Life?

E*ven if your roommate is a snoring, stingy, angry, psycho slob, the good news is that there are probably several more-or-less normal, human freshmen living close by—possibly right next door. Make sure you get to meet them.*

MAKE IT A POINT TO GET TO KNOW EVERYONE on your floor at the dorm. Invite everyone to a weekly pre-dinner cocktail party. Play some icebreaker games so that everyone gets to know everyone else. Without their old high school cliques and social circles to fall back on, most people are truly eager to meet new people and make new connections. My dorm years were phenomenal, thanks to all my fantastic floor mates.

—*LAURA WOLTER*
UNIVERSITY OF TEXAS AT AUSTIN, 1997

IF YOU PUT A THOUSAND FRESHMEN INTO A BUILDING, ANYTHING CAN AND WILL HAPPEN.

—*B.*
GEORGE WASHINGTON UNIVERSITY, SENIOR

> Dorms are not the best place for the serious student, so don't expect to get a lot of work done while at your college "home."
>
> —K. HARMA
> WESTERN
> WASHINGTON
> UNIVERSITY
> 2001

I MET MY FIRST TRUE COLLEGE FRIEND when my best friend from high school came up to visit me on Welcome Weekend. We sat with my bedroom door open and played our guitars. A girl who played guitar heard us and came by to talk. She became my first college friend.

—*AMY FORBES*
MISSISSIPPI STATE UNIVERSITY, 2003

• • • • • • • •

I WISH I'D BEEN MORE SOCIABLE. I wish I'd met more people, because now I don't really know that many people, except for my close friends. Now that everyone has gone their separate ways I don't really know any casual acquaintances or anything on campus. You form bonds in your freshman dorm and when everyone moves out and goes to other dorms, you can go see them and visit and that kind of stuff. It's kind of like a network that you can use throughout your college career. And I don't really do that.

—*T.*
STANFORD UNIVERSITY, SENIOR

• • • • • • • •

WHEN I WAS A SOPHOMORE, we had this great apartment on the top floor and we bought a huge inflatable pool about 15 feet in diameter. It had about 800 gallons of hot water from the shower. At night, in the winter, we had 101-degree water on the roof of the apartment complex, and about 20 people squeezed into this pool. I recommend that kind of ingenuity. It's not something you'll do in the real world. You don't have that kind of time to invest in your revelry once you get out of college.

—*TIM JOYCE*
GEORGETOWN UNIVERSITY, SENIOR

DORM LIFE CAN HAVE A BAD REPUTATION, but don't knock it. Everyone should have the experience. We had a blast in the freshman dorms—we had a grill on the patio, so we'd barbecue at night sometimes, especially if the cafeteria food was creepy. It's a great way to meet people—and after this year you have the rest of your life to pay your own electric bill.

—*J.I.*
SONOMA STATE UNIVERSITY, JUNIOR

• • • • • • • •

"No matter how nice your R.A. is, don't date him. It always turns out to be a bad thing—not for me, but my roommate did that."

—*KYM*
SAN JOSE STATE UNIVERSITY, SOPHOMORE

• • • • • • • •

✓ **WE WOULD ALWAYS PLAY JOKES ON EACH OTHER.** We had a suite mate who had really bad vision. One time, my roommate took her glasses when she washing her face and she couldn't find them. She was panicking. But we got my roommate back by taking all her clothes and towels while she took a shower. And when she came out, we were waiting outside with a camera. She was pissed! She was not a good sport about it.

—*S.R.I.*
CORNELL UNIVERSITY, 1994

Make sure you have good music coming out of your room since that's a good conversation starter.

—*B.K.*
CORNELL UNIVERSITY, 1996

ONE OF THE MOST IMPORTANT THINGS about surviving freshman year is that if you live in coed dorms like I did, you're going to see people in all states of life. You're going to see them on the can, you're going to see them before they've painted their face on, and you're going to have to get over the shock.

I've met long-term friends in the dorms. Everyone bonds in a totally different way when you live there. People go through difficult times—separation from family, separation from friends—and you all have that in common.

> —*ZACH FRIEND*
> *UNIVERSITY OF CALIFORNIA AT SANTA CRUZ, 2001*

• • • • • • • •

ONE OF MY FRIENDS LIVED above a group of guys who would blare music until one or two in the morning. She would go down in her pajamas and ask them to turn the music down, but they never did. So one morning when she got up at six, she opened up her windows and blared country music until she could hear them stirring and cursing.

> —*ANONYMOUS*
> *WESTERN WASHINGTON UNIVERSITY, 2001*

• • • • • • • •

DORM LIFE WAS CLAUSTROPHOBIC and suffocating. I didn't enjoy it. I'm an only child, and eventually I got a single, but even then the rooms were tight and the beds were small, and you just felt like you were running into a wall half the time. So, I got out a lot; I went out and saw friends. You adapt. It was a good experience. After that, you appreciate where you live.

> —*J.P.G.*
> *UNIVERSITY OF PENNSYLVANIA, SOPHOMORE*

DON'T MESS WITH DAVE

My freshman-year roommates and I lived across the hall from a senior, an electrical engineering/computer science major named Dave. Dave, who was a nice guy, had been really busy late in the year preparing his senior thesis: staying up real late or pulling all-nighters, and maybe getting a few hours of sleep in the mornings. One night we thought we'd have a little fun with Dave.

Dave had just bought this new car that he loved. So we put an ad in the college paper, in Dave's name, saying that due to some personal issues he had to sell this car and was basically giving it away for a ridiculously low price. Needless to say, good old Dave's phone started ringing at about 5 A.M., when the first paper hit the dorms. Some people figured out what dorm Dave lived in, based on the phone number, and started showing up at his door.

Dave wasn't too pleased. He did, however get some revenge. He figured out—remember, he was an EECS major—how to lock my roommate's computer account at the computer center (this was before everyone had their own PCs). My roommate had a hell of a time begging Dave to turn his account back on so that he could finish his own end-of-year papers.

So, if you plan to play any practical jokes on neighbors, check your back, and make sure they can't screw you worse.

—Y.K.
PRINCETON UNIVERSITY, 1980

KNOW YOUR SPACE BEFORE YOU PACK UP and arrive. One family came with a U-Haul full of stuff—a bed, desk, everything—and saw there was no room for any of it. They turned around and drove it right back home.

—TOM SABRAM
CARNEGIE MELLON UNIVERSITY, SOPHOMORE

• • • • • • • •

RESPECT YOUR ROOMMATE and don't leave pizza in the room for a week. It's not your roommate's job to throw it out. The room stinks; it's not livable. People don't want to come in your room because it stinks. And don't try to blame the bad smell on the fact that your roommate's clothes are on the floor. That is not what's causing the nasty, rotten smell in your room. That would be the pizza box that you left there for a week.

—ANONYMOUS
UNIVERSITY OF VIRGINIA, SOPHOMORE

• • • • • • • •

YOU CAN'T TRUST EVERYONE IN YOUR DORM. A girl's room was robbed by a friend of someone who lived next door. On the first day there, everybody was coming in and out and leaving their doors open so that people could come and meet everybody. Everyone was hanging out when she noticed, "Where's my phone, how come my phone is gone?" Then they noticed the stereo was missing, and 100 dollars out of someone's wallet. So they called the cops and they realized it was a friend of someone who lived next door. The guy was hiding in the closet, and the girl was pro-  tecting him. Eventually she got kicked out for hiding him, but it took a few months.

—A. TANG
UNIVERSITY OF CALIFORNIA AT BERKELEY, 2002

Top 5 Best Dorms

based on students' ranking of dorm comfort:

Loyola College (Maryland)

Smith College (Massachussetts)

Bryn Mawr College (Pennsylvania)

Scripps College (California)

Agnes Scott College (Georgia)

SET MONTHLY CLEAN-UP TIMES and stick to them. Failure to do so might result in an infestation of dust bunnies.

—*KHALIL SULLIVAN*
PRINCETON UNIVERSITY, JUNIOR

• • • • • • • •

I LIVED IN A MIXED DORM MY FRESHMAN YEAR. I was sad because I wanted to live in an all-freshman dorm, but there were these two senior guys on my hall whom I became close with. It's wonderful because they graduated and they stayed in the Bay Area; if I ever have problems or want to talk about something, they're in the real world and have a little more perspective. They influenced what classes I took as a freshman and what major I picked. I think it's important to take advantage of those resources and not be afraid to seek them out and talk to them about classes and stuff. As a freshman I thought, "Oh my gosh, they're so much older than I am." I was so intimidated. But now, as I'm going into my senior year, I see it from the other side and I want people to come talk to me; if I could help somebody the way I was helped in my freshman year by upperclassmen, that would be awesome.

—*JULIE TORRES*
STANFORD UNIVERSITY, SENIOR

• • • • • • • •

MY DORM ROOM WAS WRECKED. It was an absolute mess. I chose a dorm room where we had our own bathroom; that was a huge mistake. It got destroyed. You have a roommate and you think, "Well, maybe I'll wait for him to clean it up." But it never happens. By the end of the year, I didn't even go in there.

—*JOHNNY*
GEORGETOWN UNIVERSITY, JUNIOR

Bottom 5 Worst Dorms

based on students' ranking of dorm comfort:

University of Missouri—Rolla

University of Oregon

SUNY-Albany

Illinois Institute of Technology

Hampton University (Virginia)

WHEN I CAME TO SCHOOL, I KNEW NO ONE. I entered an all-male dorm and everyone thought we were dirty, stinky guys—and we were. With no girls around, there was no need to really focus on hygiene. But because we were so isolated, we bonded super tight and have great friendships for life. We have the last laugh: Now we can bathe, but the other folks don't have our strong friendships. All-male dorms are a good idea.

—*JUSTIN PEABODY*
CARNEGIE MELLON UNIVERSITY, JUNIOR

· · · · · · · ·

❝You have to be conscious of everyone around you. And also, living in the dorm, everyone knows about everyone else. If you do something dumb, everyone knows about it.❞

—*MAUREEN SULLIVAN*
GEORGETOWN UNIVERSITY, SOPHOMORE

· · · · · · · ·

GET TO KNOW PEOPLE ON YOUR HALL. Leave your door open when you're there. If you leave it open, people will stop by. It's a nice break from studying.

—*AMY STOUT*
GEORGIA INSTITUTE OF TECHNOLOGY, SOPHOMORE

MAKE FRIENDS WITH PEOPLE who are not on your hall. That way, when you need a break from your dorm or your roommate, you can call those people and say, "I need to get out of here, I'm coming over!" I would usually completely leave my dorm during the day. I wouldn't return to my room until the evening. That way my life didn't revolve around my hall. Find something to do by yourself outside your dorm, like biking, running, or singing; whatever it is that will get you out.

—SUMMER J.
UNIVERSITY OF VIRGINIA, SENIOR

• • • • • • • •

IF YOU'RE GOING TO LIVE IN THE DORM, I hope you like noise. Dorms are what they are advertised to be: a place to meet people and have lots of fun. Some of my best friends to this day are people I met and bonded with while trying to survive dorm life. So, if you opt for living in the dorms, expect a lot of fun and interesting experiences; just don't count on getting a lot of studying or sleep.

—K. HARMA
WESTERN WASHINGTON UNIVERSITY, 2001

• • • • • • • •

GET ALONG WITH YOUR R.A. When I was in the dorm, I always used to pull pranks on my R.A. because she was a big bitch. We broke into her room and took a bunch of stuff and put it all over the floor. It didn't go well. I had to do MADD community service for that. Don't fuck with your R.A., because you get nailed. Keep your mouth shut when it comes to authority.

—ANONYMOUS
BROWN UNIVERSITY, SOPHOMORE

Seek out the people on your floor who have installed bars in the bedrooms. They will be fun to hang out with.

—AMY FORBES
MISSISSIPPI STATE
UNIVERSITY, 2003

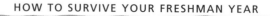

DECORATING TIPS: A WORLD OF INTERIORS

Make sure to talk to your roommate to see what you need to bring and what you don't. I talked to my roommate before I moved in but we did not discuss everything and ended up having two phones, two answering machines, and then there were many things we forgot to bring so we had to go out and buy them. And, get a rug—it's a good investment for a dorm. The floors are usually dirty and a rug at least looks cleaner.

> —*E.M.G.*
> *UNIVERSITY OF SOUTH FLORIDA, JUNIOR*

Guys, keep your rooms clean, because there will be girls in your room and they'll be turned off if you have disgusting rooms.

> —*REID ATTAWAY*
> *JAMES MADISON UNIVERSITY, SOPHOMORE*

If you're going to steal furniture for your dorm room, steal it from the lounge. They won't find it until they spray for bugs over spring break—then you only have a few weeks of classes left anyway.

—J.G.
FLORIDA STATE UNIVERSITY, 1991

• • • • • • • •

Go nuts on the decorating. Be tacky, be shocking. This is the only time in your life you can get away with hanging a beer sign in your window or assembling a Buddah shrine in your bathroom. I actually had an Elvis shrine in my bathroom.

—WENDY W.
UNIVERSITY OF GEORGIA, 1996

• • • • • • • •

Spend time making your room a place you would want to hang out in and study in. If you don't feel comfortable in your room, which is basically your college home, where are you going to feel comfortable?

—JULIE
PRINCETON UNIVERSITY, SOPHOMORE

Don't be shy.
Go up to people in your
building and
introduce
yourself.

—*Kelli*
 University of
 Delaware
 Sophomore

I HAD A FRIEND WHO HAD A VIRUS on his computer, didn't realize it, and saved something to a disk. He went to my computer. Thank God I had it turned off. He went to my friend's computer, and put the disk in. It started going crazy and completely wiped out her hard drive. He's like, "What's going on?" Her computer was completely destroyed. And he left a note: "I think something's wrong." So turn off your computer. Don't let people use it unless you're there.

—*B.*
 George Washington University, Senior

• • • • • • • •

My roommate and about three other kids on the hall unpacked their bottles of alcohol and sat around bonding on the very first night. Then we went out and wreaked havoc on the campus. We brought back a few things our R.A. wasn't very happy about. Brought back a few street signs, the head of a palm tree, and we tipped over a port-a-potty—and when you tip over a port-a-potty it all gushes out. It was disgusting. We still talk about it.

—*T.*
 Stanford University, Senior

Choosing and Surviving Your Roommates

That stranger you just met a few minutes ago is going to be sharing your living quarters for the next year. Figuring out how to live together without driving each other crazy is one of the biggest challenges you'll face in college, and can make the difference between a dream year and a nightmare. You may want to share this chapter with your roommate!

WHEN DEALING WITH YOUR DORM ROOMMATE, make sure you have an understanding about everything—boys coming over and spending the night, what time you go to bed, music; whatever. Something your roommate does might not bother you at first, but then it keeps building up, and then you get pissed off.

—*ALFIE WILLIAMS*
GEORGIA INSTITUTE OF TECHNOLOGY, SOPHOMORE

FEEL FREE TO AVOID YOUR ROOMMATE IF YOU NEED TO.
—*JOHN BENTLEY*
TRINITY UNIVERSITY, 1995

✓ **DON'T BE ROOMMATES** with your old high-school friends because then you just bond together and you don't meet other people. But if you live with a new person she'll introduce you to a whole bunch of other aspects of life. She'll open you up to a whole world you wouldn't have expected. It worked for me. It was a good experience with my roommate and I learned a lot.

—*KYM*
SAN JOSE STATE UNIVERSITY, SOPHOMORE

❝Your roommate is the first person you really get to know. After going to bed, my roommate and I would talk for about forty-five minutes about the most random things. It's the person you meet first and know the best first. You branch out from there and get to know the whole floor. ❞

—*BRYAN*
GEORGETOWN UNIVERSITY, SOPHOMORE

IF YOU HAVE A ROOMMATE WHO'S PSYCHO, don't be afraid to leave. Just go to the R.A. and get reassigned. It's a hassle, but it's better than living with a psycho.

—*S.G.*
COLUMBIA UNIVERSITY, SENIOR

YOU CAN BE INDIFFERENT TO PEOPLE you pass on your walks around campus, but if you're indifferent to your roommate, silence turns into coldness, and coldness turns into animosity, which might turn into hatred. So continue to cultivate your relationship with your roommates. Also, if you know that you are a naturally introverted person, go for a single. Many upperclassmen choose to have singles, so they must know something.

—*SEAN CAMERON*
PRINCETON UNIVERSITY, SOPHOMORE

• • • • • • • •

I LOVE MY ROOMMATE. She's my closest friend here. We talked the day after we got the rooming information and we clicked on the phone. Don't come on too strong with your roommate, and don't think you have to be friends right away. But if you do, that's great.

—*M.D.*
BOSTON COLLEGE, FRESHMAN

• • • • • • • •

BE REALLY HONEST ON YOUR ROOMMATE form or you might end up with somebody you don't get along with. It's hard to share your personal space with someone else. The space tends to be really small.

—*RUTH FEINBLUM*
BRYN MAWR COLLEGE, JUNIOR

Be honest with your roommate. You have nothing to gain by living inside a closet. No one should be made to feel uncomfortable in his or her own room.

—*J.*
BROWN UNIVERSITY JUNIOR

TRUE TO FORM

My roommate filled out the form about habits and interests with what she thought would get her the "coolest" roommate, rather than by her real habits.

The result: She smoked, I did not; she did not study with music on, I did; she woke up really early and spent an hour getting ready every morning, including major makeup mirror with intense lights that shined right in my sleeping face, and I woke up a bit later (or would have liked to), and showered and got ready in 20 minutes or so; she went to sleep really early and I did not.

Bottom line: She was from Texas and by the time Columbus Day weekend came she decided to transfer to UT where all of her friends were.

Another story: I arrived to the room first and unloaded all my stuff but did not stake a claim to a bunk (yes, bunk beds) because I thought we should discuss it so that we'd both feel it was fair. She arrived a good 6 hours after me, her mom places her purse on the bottom bunk and says, "I guess this bed is Sharon's." I was too dumbfounded and hopeful that we would get along so I let it stand. . . and was stuck on the top bunk. This meant when I went to sleep late (as my form indicated) she would complain that I was making noise getting into bed.

Karma did come back because I did not get another roommate for second semester and happily enjoyed my single!

—D.
WELLESLEY COLLEGE, 1991

FRESHMAN YEAR WAS CRAZY. It was tough to get adjusted to school life; there was a lot of partying and a lot of girls. Just say no—to everything. And if your roommate can't say no, change roommates. My roommate couldn't say no, and I couldn't say no; we just played off each other. It wasn't good.

—*KENTON*
UNIVERSITY OF VIRGINIA, SENIOR

" If your roommate is not good— for instance, if the person steals your food, throws dirty laundry on your bed, etc.—get out as soon as possible because your life will be hell. And it's easy to do that, too; just go to your R.A. "

—*K.*
NORTHWESTERN UNIVERSITY, 2001

MY FIRST ROOMMATE HAD MADE OTHER PLANS. But I got a new roommate, and it was a great experience. Sometimes you click and get along with someone. We didn't argue, and we had a lot of fun. We each had our own separate lives; our boyfriends got along. It was a great roommate setup. The lesson: If your first roommate doesn't work out for whatever reason, there's probably someone else out there who will become one of your best friends.

—*GINGER M. BRODTMAN*
SPRING HILL COLLEGE, 1998

CHECK UNDER YOUR ROOMMATE'S BED for old, moldy food. For two weeks our room completely stunk. People were avoiding my room and I was wondering, "What's going on?" I never thought to look under my roommate's bed. When I did I found an old can of salsa and moldy bread.

—*SIERRA*
CAL POLY SAN LOUIS OBISPO, JUNIOR

- - - - - - - -

It's not the end of the world if you don't get along with your room-mate.

—*KERRY*
GEORGETOWN
UNIVERSITY, 2002

I LIVED WITH MY BEST FRIEND and it was the worst thing I did my fresh-man year. We didn't speak for a year after that. It was like a competi-tion, rather than a partnership, always seeing who could make plans to do something cool, see-ing how high the dishes could stack up. At first, we did everything together, but then learned we didn't like each other's company that much and almost never talked. That's not easy when you live with someone. When the year was finally over, it was a relief. We'd had enough of each other; there was no reason to hang out.

—*IRVING BURNS RAMSOWER III*
UNIVERSITY OF FLORIDA, 1992

- - - - - - - -

THE ROOMMATE-SELECTION SURVEYS never ask questions that are meaningful enough to give you insight into how it's really going to be like to live with someone. So just expect the unexpected and get ready to be flexible. According to the survey, my freshman-year roommate appeared to be a conservative who liked country music. She turned out to be a very dynamic and wild gal who kept me laughing throughout the year.

—*K. HARMA*
WESTERN WASHINGTON UNIVERSITY, 2001

I HAD A ROOMMATE WHO HAD SEX IN THE ROOM
while I was sleeping. I thought they were just
lying there; I would hear whispering and I
thought they were just talking. Nope, they were
porking. They told me later, when they were
drunk. That's all right though, I'm okay with that.

> —*SEIJI YAMAMOTO*
> *STANFORD UNIVERSITY, 2002*

• • • • • • • •

DON'T LET PEOPLE'S FLAWS GET TO YOU SO HARD.
Everyone has flaws. If your roommate is messy,
discuss it. One friend's roommate was a total
slob. She would make macaroni and cheese,
eat half of it, and let the other half sit for a
week. I saw lemon juice curdle in her room. It
was gross!

> —*KEISHA*
> *EMORY UNIVERSITY, SENIOR*

• • • • • • • •

MY ROOMMATE THINKS I'M MESSY and I think
she's too neat. We argue over that. And we have a
division going down the middle of the room; her
stuff on one side and mine on the other.

> —*WHITNEY*
> *YALE UNIVERSITY, FRESHMAN*

• • • • • • • •

SCHEDULE MONTHLY OUTINGS with all of your
roommates. And if you pay the bill, that really
messy roommate might make an effort to clean
up after himself every now and then.

> —*KHALIL SULLIVAN*
> *PRINCETON UNIVERSITY, JUNIOR*

I WOULD ARGUE WITH MY ROOMMATE. She would tell me that I'm an obsessive-compulsive and she couldn't deal with it anymore. And I would be like, "What are you talking about, you psycho." So, I spent a lot of time in the library, which is a good thing.

—S.
UNIVERSITY OF VIRGINIA, SOPHOMORE

"Compromise with your roommate. We're each used to having our own room. It's not like she's your sister or something. It's a total stranger and you have to compromise about everything like about when you're going to listen to music; we have to take turns. It feels like summer camp at first, but then you have to realize that you're going to be here awhile."

—Z.S.
GEORGE WASHINGTON UNIVERSITY, FRESHMAN

MY FRESHMAN YEAR I ROOMED WITH A SENIOR
who was living in the dorms for the convenience,
but she had a serious boyfriend and moved out of
the room after the first week. I could hear people
through the walls laughing and getting to know
their new friend and roommate, whereas I was
staring at an empty bed the first week of college.

> —*DIANA SHU*
> *UNIVERSITY OF CALIFORNIA AT BERKELEY, SOPHOMORE*

• • • • • • • •

I HAD ROOMMATE PROBLEMS. I roomed with someone I knew from high school, but I didn't know
her well enough to know she had this drama
going on every day of her life. I had to get away
from that.

> —*ANONYMOUS*
> *JAMES MADISON UNIVERSITY, SOPHOMORE*

• • • • • • • •

✓ **LEARN HOW TO SLEEP THROUGH ALARMS.**
My roommate got up every morning at
five o'clock to go to basketball practice. Her
alarm woke me every morning for a good two
months. Get some sort of system, where you put
a pillow over your head, and then you take the
pillow off after your roommate leaves so you can
hear your own alarm.

> —*CATE*
> *BROWN UNIVERSITY, JUNIOR*

• • • • • • • •

I HAD A ROOMMATE WHO SNORED and I had to go
to the study lounge to sleep. I would take my
blanket and comforter and sleep on a couch or
chair at two in the morning. I got out the second
semester. I didn't have the heart to tell him. Other
than the snoring, we got along great.

> —*RICK SHILLING*
> *PENN STATE UNIVERSITY, 1998*

WE WERE CHOOSING ROOMMATES ONE YEAR, and we felt really sorry for this one guy, so we let him draw with us. But in the end it was worse for us and worse for him. We would have been better off just saying, "Look, we don't get along with you, you don't get along with us. It's not a good idea." We just had more and more clashes over the course of the year.

—*KHALED HASSAN*
STANFORD UNIVERSITY, JUNIOR

• • • • • • • •

WE HAD A BAD ROOMMATE THE FIRST YEAR. He was really unstable; he would go from loving us one minute to hating us the next. He was really inconsiderate to our neighbors and friends. After a couple of months, we had to go to the building director and have him thrown out.

—*PAUL HEITHOFF*
GEORGE WASHINGTON UNIVERSITY, SOPHOMORE

• • • • • • • •

I'M IN A TRIPLE. What happens in a triple is that two people combine and go off together. And that's what happened with me; I'm the odd one out. But I don't feel bad about it because they're not my kind of people.

—*AMY HOFFBERG*
UNIVERSITY OF DELAWARE, FRESHMAN

• • • • • • • •

WHEN I STARTED COLLEGE, I was under the impression that a roommate was a temporary assignment, much like week-long summer camps. However, after a few weeks of living with the most miserable person ever imagined, I came to realize that he didn't seem to be going away. In college it's important to be comfortable with your living arrangements: If you're unhappy, tell someone.

—*ANONYMOUS*

IN ORDER TO SURVIVE YOUR ROOMMATES, you have to be friendly and considerate. If you are nice, you will get treated the same way (and if you don't, then you have a reason to be treated like a jerk). Some people like living alone in singles, but I enjoy a crowd. Sure, it makes hooking up tricky (and hilarious) sometimes, but it also expands your social circle, and gives you lifelong friends— or enemies! It all depends on what kind of person you are.

—*PETE*
PRINCETON UNIVERSITY, SOPHOMORE

• • • • • • • •

MY LAST ROOMMATE'S BOYFRIEND tried to move in with us. He had gotten kicked out of his dorm and was a troublemaker, dealing drugs. I'm very passive, but I had to stand up for myself and voice my opinion, even though that's kind of difficult for me. I said, "That's not fair, you can't do this." He was there all the time, his stuff was in our room all the time. And when they fought, it would be really awkward. They'd cuss each other out and scream. So, I just went to the R.A. and the boyfriend got banned from our dorm. But we worked everything out and in the end it was fine.

—*A.*
JAMES MADISON UNIVERSITY, SOPHOMORE

• • • • • • • •

DORM LIVING IS PROBABLY GOOD FOR ME. It's different. I'm going to meet a lot of different people, and I'm going to have to deal with a lot of different lifestyles. I think one of my roommates is homosexual, and now we have another one moving in, and I don't know if I really feel comfortable with that—it's weird for me just because of the way I was raised. I just have to adapt, and that may take a while.

—*ANONYMOUS*
GEORGIA STATE UNIVERSITY, FRESHMAN

MY ROOMMATE AND **I** HAVE A BIG DIFFERENCE in music tastes. I listen to rock and alternative, and she listens to this really bad R&B all the time. Whoever gets to the room first gets to choose the radio; sometimes it's a dash from class back to the room.

—*ANONYMOUS*
YALE UNIVERSITY, SOPHOMORE

• • • • • • • •

I WALKED INTO MY ROOM FOR THE FIRST TIME freshman year to see that my roommate had decorated my side of the room with posters, a hanging thing over my bed, and the quote "G-d is dead" on the eraser board. That night I took everything down because I wanted to put up my own stuff. That was the start of our amazing roommate relationship. Oh, and the fact that her boyfriend lived in my room. My survival was pledging a sorority, so I was never there.

—*M.*
AMERICAN UNIVERSITY, FRESHMAN

• • • • • • • •

I WOULDN'T WANT TO GO BACK to the living conditions I was in freshman year. You can learn a lot, but it's aggravating when you have to deal with someone who doesn't blend with your personality. For instance, I'm not real neat, but my roommate freshman year was a real neat freak. We had our problems there. Don't bend over backwards for your roommate, but there are sacrifices you have to make. When you say "compromise," it sounds like you have to lose something to make the other person happy. Instead, you find a way to make it a win-win situation.

—*BRIAN*
JAMES MADISON
UNIVERSITY, JUNIOR

Give your roommate his space, and he should give you yours.

—*DANIEL RUSK*
UNIVERSITY OF
MARYLAND
SOPHOMORE

NEAT NERDS WELCOME

My roommate smoked Dunhills all day. There were piles of ashes under his bed; it was disgusting. He left stuff strewn about, so I was always kicking shit back to his side of the room. At first appearance he seemed cool, like someone I would get along with. He was a wrestler, really into writing, but he was a dud and really unmotivated to do well—or do anything— in school. I tried not to confront him, but there were times when he'd be up late— making noise or smoking—and I was the one who would be getting up for class in the morning. I do recall one run-in, where there was a little pushing involved. Beware of kids who taunt you and don't respect your privacy. You may not appreciate it on day one, but you'll be happy with a soft-spoken, class-attending roommate. It's tough to find someone in sync with you. You may think you want to room with someone who on paper appears to be like you, but it could be misery living with him or her.

—J.
COLUMBIA UNIVERSITY, 1986

MY ROOMMATE AND I TALKED VIA EMAIL before we came to school. We realized we had a lot in common. We both play guitar and we were both bringing acoustic guitars. Then we got here and we realized we both have completely different tastes in music. But we get along really well. We compromise really well. If it's time to clean the room, we don't fight about it. One of us volunteers and it gets done.

—*REID ATTAWAY*
JAMES MADISON UNIVERSITY, FRESHMAN

66Keep an open mind. I talked to my roommate on the phone and I was totally convinced that I wasn't going to like her. She sounded like a person who was very different from me, but now she's one of my best friends. I was lucky it worked out that way. People came and hung out in our room and stayed on our futons. It was a great time.99

—*LAUREN*
GEORGETOWN UNIVERSITY, SOPHOMORE

USE YOUR INGENUITY TO GET A GOOD ROOMMATE.

When you are listing what you are like in the application for roommates, be honest. I know a guy who pretended to be a "stay in and study" kind of guy, and he got stuck with a roomie who never left the room and had a sleeping disorder. If he had been honest and said he liked to party this would not have happened. If you get a bad roommate get out of it before it gets worse. The longer you wait, the harder it is.

—*JUDSON KROH*
CARNEGIE MELLON UNIVERSITY, JUNIOR

• • • • • • • •

✓ **I WAS TOLD I WOULD HAVE JUST ONE ROOMMATE** my freshman year. Little did I know I'd have a permanent visitor: my roommate's boyfriend. He was like "the guy on the couch"; he would stay Friday to Wednesday, always on the couch, on my computer, or even on my bed when I came home from class. Although I was open to guests, I had to tell my roommate I was sick of having a dude in my space all the time. It didn't go down well. Soon she moved down the hall into a single; she set up her very own love nest.

—*LISA G.*
NEW YORK UNIVERSITY, JUNIOR

• • • • • • • •

THE OTHER DAY, MY ROOMMATE ASKED ME to

leave the room. I asked why. He said, "You know." He wanted to be alone, if you know what I mean. So I left, for like an hour. That's one of the things you have to put up with when you have a roommate.

—*C.*
COLUMBIA UNIVERSITY, JUNIOR

> Freshmen, realize that you're going to spend enough time with your roommates anyway, so it's not necessary that they come with you wherever you go.
>
> —*ANONYMOUS*
> *UNIVERSITY OF VIRGINIA SOPHOMORE*

Become good friends with your R.A. He or she could be nice, and may one day help you lock your horrible roommate into the room with pennies.

—ANONYMOUS
MICHIGAN
TECHNOLOGICAL
UNIVERSITY, 2002

I'VE ALWAYS BEEN SOMETHING OF A MAMA'S BOY. She was always great about picking up after me and everything. By the end of my fall quarter, my room looked like a hurricane had come through and then came through again. It was God-awful; it was a nasty pigsty. My roommate was a neat freak, but he was pretty cool with it.

—F.
STANFORD UNIVERSITY, SOPHOMORE

. . . .

I DIDN'T GET ALONG WELL WITH THE GIRL I lived with freshman year. We fought; we hated each other. I thought she was actually Satan. She had massive mood swings, and there was no telling what was going to kick them off. I think she was on a lot of different strange drugs; those might have affected her moods. I left the room as often as possible and I tried to stay out of her way. But we're friends now.

—ANONYMOUS
UNIVERSITY OF VIRGINIA, SOPHOMORE

. . . .

MY ROOMMATES WERE ALL FROM THE DEEP SOUTH. One of them was the daughter of an Episcopalian minister. We got into some clashes. She told me that I was going to hell, in all seriousness. She was concerned for my soul. So, I didn't have any-one to talk to about that. But other than that it was fine. I had some friends who went to a bigger college nearby, and I would drive an hour and a half to hang out with them there.

—HANNAH SMITH
HARVARD UNIVERSITY, JUNIOR

. . . .

MY ROOMMATE IS MY TWIN SISTER. I get along with her. We know how to live together; my sister does the laundry and I clean the room.

—MANI
UNIVERSITY OF MARYLAND, FRESHMAN

MY ROOMMATE CAME WITH ONE BAG TO SCHOOL, he didn't have any sheets for his bed, he had this long beard that he used to cut in the sink and it got everywhere. He was a wreck. He couldn't be more different from me and the other guys in our suite. I tried to be friends with him, but it became clear that we were opposite personalities. So we agreed to disagree. He wasn't so bad that I couldn't live there, but I spent a lot of time out with my friends and every once a while showed up there to sleep.

—JOHN BENTLEY
TRINITY UNIVERSITY, 1995

. . . .

I HAD ARRANGED TO BE ROOMMATES with a high school friend—and the adage that you don't know someone until you live with them really applies. They may do things that you find bothersome, and if you weren't living with them, these characteristics may not have been revealed. So I recommend not rooming with someone you've known previously.

—YALDA A.
UNIVERSITY OF CALIFORNIA AT BERKELEY, 2002

. . . .

MY ROOMMATE SMOKED ALL THE TIME and she was such a slob and I'm so not a slob. Most people haven't shared rooms when they get to college. It's the first time they've ever done that, and they suck at it. I grew up sharing a room with my sister. You have to learn how to compromise, or you're not going to make it through the year alive.

—B.
JAMES MADISON UNIVERSITY, SENIOR

ONE OF MY ROOMMATES WAS VERY CONSERVATIVE, very traditional. The other was this vegan lesbian. They were both wonderful people, but it was interesting to be occasionally mediating between the two.

—*MELISSA K. BYRNES*
AMHERST COLLEGE, 2000

• • • • • • • •

Some people make great friends, and some people make great roommates.

—*YALDA A.*
UNIVERSITY OF CALIFORNIA AT BERKELEY, 2002

FIND OUT WHO YOUR ROOMMATE IS before you come—and check him out. If he is not a good fit, get out of it. If you complain loud enough, they will swap him for you. This is great advice.

—*DEREK LI*
CARNEGIE MELLON UNIVERSITY, JUNIOR

• • • • • • • •

SPEAK UP WHEN YOUR ROOMMATE or suitemate does something you can't stand. One suitemate in particular left her dirty underwear in the bathroom, had loud sex late at night, and was totally filthy and horrible. I went to her room twice to shut up her and her pals (all underage) when they were drinking in her room at three o'clock on a school night. The rest I tried to forget, but it never went away. The R.A. never knew enough about what was going on in the hall.

—*ANONYMOUS*
MICHIGAN TECHNOLOGICAL UNIVERSITY, 2002

• • • • • • • •

IT'S HARD BEING SICK WITH A ROOMMATE. You have to share this really small space. I once had this health-nut roommate who was a germophobe. That was really bad. Every time I got sick, she would open doors with a Kleenex. What was I supposed to do? I couldn't go home.

—*KAIT DUNTON*
UNIVERSITY OF VIRGINIA, JUNIOR

Filling the Daytime Hours: Choosing Classes

This may come as a surprise, but most colleges actually expect you to spend some time learning—well, at least attending class. You may not go very often, but you've got to sign up. Sure, you'll study the course catalog to see what looks good. Or, you'll ask friends and read this chapter for the real inside scoop.

GO FOR THE GOOD TEACHERS and the bad times instead of the good times and bad teachers. I took calculus the first semester at 8 a.m. and that time just sucked. But I had a good teacher and I got an A. Second semester, I took a class at 1 P.M. and it was a hard teacher, and I got a C.

—*AMY SCEVIOUR*
GEORGIA INSTITUTE OF TECHNOLOGY, SOPHOMORE

MAKE YOUR OWN PATH AND FIND YOUR OWN TEACHERS.

—*EBELE ONYEMA*
GEORGETOWN UNIVERSITY, SENIOR

FALL IN LOVE WITH SOMEONE IN YOUR CLASS RIGHT AWAY; student, T.A., professor, whomever. You'll be hard-pressed to skip class. If there is no one in your class to love, then pick someone to hate and show up every day to make his or her life a living hell.

—S.P.
UNIVERSITY OF GEORGIA, 1999

• • • • • • •

66 Never sign up for a 7 a.m. class. Yes, you did it in high school, but Mom was always there to keep waking you up, and if by some miracle you do make it to an early class, you will sleep through the lecture when you get there. 99

—J.T.
UNIVERSITY OF FLORIDA, 1990

• • • • • • • •

MOST PEOPLE JUST DO SCHOOL—you don't see a lot of students doing research, playing sports, doing extra-curricular activities—and one can sense the monotony. I suggest you take the perspective that grades don't count and take classes with professors who are passionate about what they're teaching. Learn, don't just take classes that you think will yield a higher grade.

—YALDA A.
UNIVERSITY OF CALIFORNIA AT BERKELEY, 2002

IF YOU KNOW SOME PEOPLE who are already at your college, talk to them and see which professors are good and which ones suck.

> —*ANDREW OUZTS*
> *GEORGIA INSTITUTE OF TECHNOLOGY, SOPHOMORE*

• • • • • • • •

I WOULD RECOMMEND THAT during your first year, you take a class that is outside what you think you want to do. You'll meet other people, and freshman year is a really good time to meet a lot of people. Take the P.E. classes; it's something active. If you're in a very academic school, go out and have something active in your life. It's a good release. I did martial arts—Tai Kwon Do. That was really fun and you meet a lot of different people there. And kick some ass.

> —*JASPER*
> *UNIVERSITY OF CALIFORNIA AT BERKELEY, JUNIOR*

• • • • • • • •

DON'T BELIEVE PEOPLE when they tell you a professor is really good. They're probably wrong. I've taken about three classes because someone told me the professor was so cool and so good, and those are the three classes I hated the most. Then I hated the people that recommended the classes to me. Find the classes that interest you, and you'll be fine.

> —*EBELE ONYEMA*
> *GEORGETOWN UNIVERSITY, SENIOR*

• • • • • • • •

JUST BECAUSE SOME PEOPLE DON'T GO TO CLASS and still get A's doesn't mean you can skip class and still get A's. You can try it, but I wouldn't recommend it.

> —*J.D.*
> *EMORY UNIVERSITY, SENIOR*

Take the most interesting and easiest classes you can find, have a good time, and try not to flunk out.

> —*JUAN GONZALEZ*
> *CLEMSON*
> *UNIVERSITY, 1988*

ONE OF THE DUMBEST THINGS I did my first semester was taking my Dad's advice on classes. It went something like this: "Well, son, you might as well take 8 a.m. classes every day to get it out of the way. You've been doing it in school for the last 12 years. It won't be any different." What a mistake. The last thing you want to do in college is get up for an 8 a.m. class. It's easier to "get it out of the way" by sleeping right through it. I advise beginning classes no sooner than 10:30 a.m.

—*J.G.*
FLORIDA STATE UNIVERSITY, 1991

• • • • • • • •

ACADEMICALLY, TRY TO GET TO KNOW PROFESSORS. Don't get caught in the trap that he's some guy in the Emerald City hiding behind the curtain. Your professor is just a person.

—*PHIL*
UNIVERSITY OF VIRGINIA, SENIOR

• • • • • • • •

When studying Far East religions, don't confuse a llama with the Dalai Lama, the spiritual leader of Tibet.

—*LYNN LAMOUSIN*
LOUISIANA STATE UNIVERSITY, 1988

THE THING THAT STANDS OUT THE MOST about my freshman year is the fact that I was completely responsible for my learning. No one cared if I came to class or not; no one cared if I took notes or studied for a test. I remember thinking that it was wonderful to have so much freedom, and if the professors didn't care, why should I? I took full advantage of having no attendance phone calls, no conduct grades, no authoritarian instructors. By the time I figured out that I was wasting my time (and my parents' money) and that I had to take responsibility for my education, it wasn't too late, but my GPA never fully recovered.

—*S.A.S.*
UNIVERSITY OF SOUTH FLORIDA, 1985

✓ **FROM AN ACADEMIC PERSPECTIVE,** I would advise freshmen to use that first year as your sandbox year. It's really important. It's OK to screw off. It's OK to go out and experiment.

> —*W.J.F.*
> *GEORGETOWN UNIVERSITY, JUNIOR*

• • • • • • • •

DON'T OVERLOAD; don't take too many classes. I took too many classes. I was staying up to five and six o'clock in the morning, missing classes that morning. That's not fun.

> —*ALBERT SO*
> *GEORGIA INSTITUTE OF TECHNOLOGY, SOPHOMORE*

• • • • • • • •

GO TO EVERY CLASS; that's half the battle. If you do, you'll pass. I went to the majority of classes freshman year, but I would've done so much better if I had gone to all of them.

> —*KRISTIN THOMAS*
> *JAMES MADISON UNIVERSITY, JUNIOR*

• • • • • • • •

EVERYBODY'S SMART IN COLLEGE. At least give yourself a semester before you dive into the hard classes. I was in the top ten percent of my high school class and I felt real good about myself. But it took me the first year of college to realize I had to work real hard to make good grades.

> —*JONATHAN COHEN*
> *EMORY UNIVERSITY, SENIOR*

• • • • • • • •

STAY LATE AFTER CLASS and ask questions. It's good to be known by your professors; later on you'll need recommendations from them. It's important that you did more than just get a good grade, that your professor remembers you.

> —*JAWAN AYER-COLE, M.D.*
> *FLORIDA A&M UNIVERSITY, 1994*

Share your school supplies with fellow classmates. Believe me, there's going to be a time when you forget something in the future, so volunteer your extras.

> —*J.S.*
> *UNIVERSITY OF GEORGIA, 1995*

☆

I WAS TOTALLY INTIMIDATED BY MY CLASSES and professors. Everyone gets really hyped up about getting all A's in science classes. I let that stress me out more than my actual workload.

Eventually, I got more confident and did my own thing and stopped worrying about what other people were getting on their exams.

—*LEAH PRICE*
GEORGETOWN UNIVERSITY, SOPHOMORE

• • • • • • • •

KNOW WHICH CLASSES TO SKIP, and which classes not to skip. This is really a key point, because some professors don't care one way or another if you show up for class. All they care about is your test and homework performance. There are other professors who are sticklers for attendance, and even if you are an A student you can end up with a C, because of poor attendance.

—*TONYA BANKS*
MIAMI UNIVERSITY, 1999

• • • • • • • •

I RECOMMEND TAKING A PSYCHOLOGY CLASS. I'm taking psychology right now and it's my favorite class. I like learning about people's development.

—*STEPH*
DIABLO VALLEY COLLEGE, FRESHMAN

• • • • • • • •

TAKE A WIDE VARIETY OF CLASSES. You may find that you are interested in a subject you hadn't previously considered. Plus, freshman year is the best time to experiment with that sort of thing. And before you decide to take a certain class, make sure you know something about the professor teaching it. Ask around, search the Web; anything. A good or bad professor can genuinely make or break a class.

—*DANIELLE FRIEDMAN*
DUKE UNIVERSITY, SENIOR

I wish I'd paid more attention freshman year to what classes I was taking. Ask people what the best class they've ever taken is. Ask around.

—*SUMMER J.*
UNIVERSITY OF VIRGINIA, SENIOR

SLAVE OF APHRODITE

At the beginning of my freshman year, I was hit by Cupid's arrow. It was a direct hit—for the entire semester I was in love with my Introduction to Classical Studies professor.

Professor, whom I referred to reverently as "the 13th Olympian Goddess," taught an auditorium full of undergraduates about the follies, jealousies, battles, and—most prominently—the sex lives of Greek gods and mortals alike. I had always loved Greek mythology, but this class brought excitement and legitimacy to my obsessive hobby. I had read Catullus in my Latin class in high school, so I thought I was fully prepared for the unique and bizarre proclivities covered in my professor's 101 class, but those depraved Greeks and Romans surprised me time and time again! I think I was most surprised that this racy curriculum was discussed and taught in public! Can she talk about what seems clear to be the origins of NAMBLA at the podium?

Not all of Classical Studies was NC-17; I figure that a taste now and then kept the coeds awake and returning each week. But I loved all of it: The philosophy, the art, the architecture, the myths and poetry. Sappho, Euripides, Ovid, and Herodotus. I was hooked, to the class and to the deity who posed as our teacher. Vivid memories of hiding behind kiosks and trees while watching her every move attest to my naiveté and somewhat unhealthy fixation.

Once the semester ended, I pored over the class listings, hoping to fill my schedule with more classics and more chances to listen and catch glimpses of my professor. Alas, she was only teaching graduate classes, so my first encounter with the 13th Olympian Goddess turned out to be my last. However, I remained smitten with the subject and decided to join the Classics Department.

—PHIL CARMEL
UNIVERSITY COLLEGE–SALFORD (ENGLAND), 1985

GET TO KNOW YOUR TEACHERS, because when it comes down to getting a better final grade you might need a little help. And if your professors know you, they might be willing to help you.

—*MATT BURLESON*
UNIVERSITY OF TENNESSEE AT MARTIN, 2001

• • • • • • • •

I STARTED WITH FIVE CLASSES and I dropped three of them. I just wanted to make it as easy as possible. I had a hard time adjusting: I traveled from the West Coast to the East Coast to go to college. So I didn't put too much pressure on myself and just took what I thought I could handle.

—*COLIN O'CONNOR*
GEORGETOWN UNIVERSITY, JUNIOR

• • • • • • • •

"Choose your classes based on the professor instead of the class description."

—*ROBIN JALEEL*
EMORY UNIVERSITY, 2002

• • • • • • • •

I'M USUALLY THE TYPE OF PERSON who does all his work, but now, I actually have to think. The workload isn't harder, but it's different. I take a lot more notes now. I'm in a study skills class and they suggest a system for taking notes— dividing the page into three sections, writing notes in one part, cues for main ideas in the other, and summaries in the other. I don't like that system, but it helps to try different things.

—*DUSTIN CAMAC*
UNIVERSITY OF DELAWARE, FRESHMAN

MANY FRESHMAN CLASSES ARE HUGE, so it might be hard to let the professor know that you exist. To counter this, follow the advice everyone tells you: don't be late, and take notes. Someone gave me advice about note taking and said that if you hate it, then just bring in a tape recorder and tape the lecture. So I did and yes, it was easy, but I never listened to the tapes; or if I did, it was always a crappy recording.

In some classes they don't take attendance, which might make you feel more like not going. But it feels good if you go anyway, and you never know if you'll miss a day with a pop quiz or extra credit. As you get more focused on your major, the classes get smaller. Be involved and know your professors; ask them for advice and talk to them.

> —*LESLIE M.*
> *UNIVERSITY OF FLORIDA, 1995*

. . . .

DON'T TAKE MORE THAN ONE CLASS that has a lot of reading. I picked some classes that had too much reading, so I am always reading. I average four hours a day, maybe longer. I go to class, take a break, go to dinner, and then go to the library. I'll be in the library until 1 a.m.

> —*BAYLESS PARSLEY*
> *UNIVERSITY OF VIRGINIA, FRESHMAN*

. . . .

I TOOK COURSES THAT WERE HARDER, not what normal freshmen took. I ended up not doing as well as I should have. There's no harm taking a class you've taken already in high school. Because freshman year is about getting used to your environment, and if you're studying all the time, it's harder to do that.

> —*NATASHA PIRZADA*
> *GEORGETOWN UNIVERSITY, SOPHOMORE*

Take the opportunity to participate in class. Never again in your life will you be confronted with such an open forum for sharing ideas; this is the time to develop your skills to make a persuasive point.

> —*SCOTT WOELFEL*
> *UNIVERSITY OF*
> *MISSOURI, 1981*

AND THE MORAL OF THE STORY IS. . .

There was one class I had when I gave a big speech to the whole class, while hung over. That was a bad idea. I had an economics professor who picked out a few people to give speeches; to teach his class, basically. The night before, I got pretty drunk. The speech was on Milton Friedman's theory on something or other. I was so hung over when I tried to give the speech, I couldn't talk; I just mumbled. The professor asked me questions: "Do you mean this means that?" I said, "Yeah, yeah, that. Yes, of course." And so we got through the whole thing, and afterwards he pulled me aside and said, "Wow, I've been teaching this class for 20 years, and that is the worst description I've ever heard." And yet, I passed the class. I talked to the professor. I realized I screwed up, and I made up for it. So the moral is, if you screw up, talk your way through it. Don't let it lie. People understand.

—ANONYMOUS
UNIVERSITY OF TEXAS, 1990

✓ **HAVE A FUN CLASS.** If you're taking five classes—which is a lot of work, a lot more than the seven you took in high school—make sure that at least one of them is fun, easy, or an English class where you get to read novels.

If the first class of the semester is boring, drop it! If a professor can't make the first twenty minutes of the first class exciting, it is going to be a long semester. Go into add/drop week with a list of possible classes to take. Go to seven or eight classes in a week, or more. Then choose the best of those. It makes for a hectic week, but it will make the semester so much better.

Sometimes it's hard to get the classes you want as a freshman. But if you walk up to a professor after class and talk to him or her, tell them you really want to be in that class, and if you keep showing up, the professor will see that you are dedicated, and chances are, you'll be let into the class.

—*SUMMER J.*
UNIVERSITY OF VIRGINIA, SENIOR

• • • • • • • •

GEOLOGY (AKA "ROCKS AND JOCKS") is much harder than the course description would lead you to believe.

—*LYNN LAMOUSIN*
LOUISIANA STATE UNIVERSITY, 1988

• • • • • • • •

⭐ **MAKE YOUR PROFESSORS THINK YOU CARE** about their class. Get to know them one on one. Stay after, go to their office hours; even if you don't give a rat's ass about their class, make them think that you care.

—*BRETT STRICKLAND*
GEORGIA STATE UNIVERSITY, SOPHOMORE

YOU WANT TO GET CLASSES where you know you're going to know people so you don't have to worry about feeling weird the first couple of days.

—*KEVIN BUSHEY*
GEORGIA STATE UNIVERSITY, FRESHMAN

. . . .

I TOOK INTRODUCTION TO BUSINESS. We had routine, online quizzes on the Wall Street Journal. They were weekly and worth 10 points each. I got 7 out of 10 on the first quiz and I panicked and did not know what to do. One of my friends said to go to the T.A.'s office hours. She said this because it was a huge class and the professor didn't know who you were. My friend also suggested I sit in the front row of the class. I then went to the T.A.'s office hours and she said, "Sarah, don't worry about it. I am happy that you are showing dedication by coming to my hours." A few minutes later, the professor walked in and said to my T.A., "How are your students in the section?" She said, "They're fine, and by the way this is Sarah Fass; she was concerned about her quizzes." My professor said, "Oh, I know who she is. She sits in the front of my class. And by the way don't worry about the quiz, just keep sitting in the front row."

—*SARAH FASS*
AMERICAN UNIVERSITY, FRESHMAN

. . . .

IT'S ESSENTIAL THAT YOU BUILD UP A grade cushion in your first year. That way when you're a junior or a senior and things get tough, you don't have to worry as much about your G.P.A.

—*YAP*
NEW YORK UNIVERSITY, JUNIOR

ONE OF MY STRANGEST MEMORIES is attending a class
taught by a dead man. One of the freshman-level
psychology courses consisted of videotaped lectures
from a professor who died in the 1960s. I don't
remember his full name but his first name was Fred,
so everyone called him—you guessed it—Dead Fred.
I wish I had a picture of 500 students all staring at
small monitors streaming a flickering, grainy, black-
and-white, talking head three times a week. Maybe it
was all just one big psychology experiment.

—SCOTT WOELFEL
UNIVERSITY OF MISSOURI, 1981

ON THE DOUBLE 101

At the U.S. Coast Guard Academy, before you begin
your studies, you have to survive Swab Summer, a
seven-week "traditional military indoctrination...
designed to help young civilian students transition into
the Academy 'lifestyle.'" The training process includes
general military skills, physical conditioning, seamanship,
swimming, and—oh yes—academics. And forget about
sleeping in after a tough day: morning formations are at
that oh-so-friendly 6:20 hour.

IF PROFESSORS GIVE OUT EMAIL ADDRESSES, use
them! Don't send anything raunchy, even if you
are in love with your English professor. Use it to
communicate about class work. Email them if
you happen to have skipped class and want to
know what you have missed. This is a sure way
to win points with them. By humanizing them,
you make them a friend. I have done this a few
times and they seem to like it when you are
involved in school, even when you are not.

—EDIE SHERMAN
KINGSBOROUGH COMMUNITY COLLEGE, SENIOR

YOU'VE GOT TO FOLLOW THE GOOD FEELING. Hopefully the professors are going to be sensitive to that. If it feels good to study certain things, follow that.

—STEVE BAKER
COLUMBIA UNIVERSITY, SENIOR

• • • • • • •

TAKE CLASSES THAT YOU ACTUALLY LIKE, that you're actually interested in. Everyone I know is taking all these intense classes in subjects that they're not interested in, and they're miserable. But I'm having a great time.

—LUCY LINDSEY
HARVARD UNIVERSITY, FRESHMAN

• • • • • • •

66Do not take an easy teacher who's boring. I'm in one of those classes this semester. I find it so much better if you like the teacher and it's a tough class than if you dislike the teacher and it's easy.99

—M.M.
BOSTON COLLEGE, JUNIOR

• • • • • • •

ALL THE GOOD STUFF YOU DO ACADEMICALLY, you do in your junior and senior years. So, try to do all the crap in your freshman and sophomore years. Get it out of the way so you can enjoy your last two years.

—ANONYMOUS
JOHNS HOPKINS UNIVERSITY, JUNIOR

YOU. WILL. TEACH. ME.

One thing I learned my freshman year is that teachers don't have to have their Master's degree to teach; they just need to have one in progress. That's good for them because the school usually pays for it, but bad for the students because it means the professor doesn't already know everything he's going to be teaching you and will often be distracted by his own studies.

It's important to make sure your teacher actually knows more than you. Be brutal. Ask a million questions. I can't tell you how frustrating it is to be paying over $300 a class and hear, "I'll have to look that one up," in response to a question you already know the answer to.

Don't be afraid to be very, very mean to your teacher. Bad teachers waste your time and should not be there. You have to believe they have no feelings and drive them the hell out.

Don't let your teacher be a slacker and don't let him forget things. This should be dealt with according to the size of the college and the amount of students. For the love of sweet Jesus, my class was the only one my teacher taught, and he'd sometimes forget his notes!

By the way, the best teachers don't use notes.

—STEVEN COY
SAN DIEGO STATE UNIVERSITY, SOPHOMORE

I WENT TO A JEWISH PRIVATE HIGH SCHOOL and we were in classes from morning until night. We still had a lot of work, but not like college. In college, we have classes a couple of hours a day and the same amount of work. Freshman year, I felt like I was falling off the cliff with all the work. But I got used to it.

—CHANA WEINER
BARNARD COLLEGE, SOPHOMORE

● ● ● ● ● ● ●

LEARN A LANGUAGE. If you've taken a language in high school, take more of the same and become fluent. If not, learn a new language, but think about one you might actually use. Even if you aren't thinking about a term abroad, pick a language and go for it.

—ANONYMOUS
UNION COLLEGE

● ● ● ● ● ● ●

HONESTLY, I DON'T KNOW HOW I SURVIVED my freshman year; it was an act of God, I think . . . I remember a lot of lectures that allowed me to catch up on sleep.

—ALIX FIELD
SYRACUSE UNIVERSITY, 1991

Studying: Why, When, and How

N^o parents to tell you what to do—or what not to do. No one asking whether you did your homework or telling you to turn off the TV. So how should you get the work done? Isn't the library where you go to scout out your weekend date? Aren't those study carrels and armchairs great for a quick nap? When and where should you crack the books? Here are a few tricks.

DON'T READ IN YOUR BED; you'll fall asleep. I would read in my bed and I would, obviously, fall asleep. When you're in your bed, that's what you do. And then you start to associate reading with sleeping, so anytime you try to read anywhere, you fall asleep. So, don't read in your bed.

—BETHANY
JAMES MADISON UNIVERSITY, SENIOR

SLEEP A LOT. AND ALWAYS GO TO CLASS.

—SARAH
GEORGIA INSTITUTE OF TECHNOLOGY, 2002

Buy beaten-up, used books that have been highlighted and have notes in the margins: Instant Cliff's Notes!

—*JEN*
UNIVERSITY OF GEORGIA, 1996

I HAD A PROFESSOR TELL ME ONE TIME that the workload in college is like shoveling snow. If you do a little bit every day, you'll get by. If you wait until everything piles up, it becomes an impossible task.

—*NICHOLAS BONAWITZ*
UNIVERSITY OF ROCHESTER, 2001

• • • • • • • •

THE MAP IS NOT THE JOURNEY and the notes are not the course. Take notes but don't try to be a stenographer. Use class notes to enhance your understanding of the course; for example, flagging areas for follow-up in text or with the instructor.

—*SCOTT WOELFEL*
UNIVERSITY OF MISSOURI, 1981

• • • • • • • •

"Leave your room when you study. With all the computers and stereos and TVs nowadays, it's so hard to get work done when you're sitting there."

—*TAYLOR*
UNIVERSITY OF MARYLAND, SOPHOMORE

• • • • • • • •

WAKE UP EARLY AND STUDY. Even if you're not a morning person, make yourself one. It's the quietest time in the dorm and you'll be so productive.

—*SEAN CAMERON*
PRINCETON UNIVERSITY, SOPHOMORE

THE PROBLEM I HAD WAS THE PRIORITIZATION. You have a lot more free time in college than in high school. But you think you have more free time than you actually have. And by November of freshman year, you're behind. I don't know anyone who wasn't behind. You tend to forget to study when you first get here. You have parties, freedom from parents—you almost forget that you're in school. Freshman year, people would go to 60 to 70 percent of classes, at best, because you would stay up late and then miss morning classes. You almost forget how important education is. You worked for 12 years to get here, but just because you're here, the work doesn't stop.

—ZAK AMCHISLAVSKY
GEORGETOWN UNIVERSITY, SENIOR

• • • • • • • •

FRESHMEN COME IN AND EXPECT TO GET AN A. But then you realize you were a big fish in a small pond in high school, and in college there's a bunch of other big fish and you've got to step it up a notch.

—K.K.
NORTHWESTERN UNIVERSITY, 1998

• • • • • • • •

COLLEGE IS NOT HIGH SCHOOL; it requires you to think in very different ways than one is used to. Find one place on campus where you can study without being interrupted, and designate a portion of your time for that purpose. When reading, read for content, and know what you are reading (it makes skimming that much more effective). If you must cram, going to bed earlier and waking up at 6 a.m. to force a few more hours in is more effective, because at least you are awake for the test. But then again, that's just me.

—AMY
PRINCETON UNIVERSITY, FRESHMAN

Don't study too hard freshman year. It gets harder later.

—MADIHA SHAKIR
EMORY UNIVERSITY
2000

The self-discipline is the toughest thing. You have to set up time to study.

—Z.S.
GEORGE WASHINGTON UNIVERSITY FRESHMAN

I USED TO GO TO THE LIBRARY and when I finished studying, I thought everyone needed to finish studying, so I started throwing cheeseballs and making noise. Because of the noise in the library they hired monitors, and because of my experience, I was hired. But I couldn't resist my basic tendencies: I was relegated to a position in the basement.

—JOEL ROSENFELD
UNIVERSITY OF CHICAGO, 1979

• • • • • • • •

IF YOU'RE QUESTIONING whether or not to go to a party, you better not go to that party, you know what I'm saying? Kids in college don't have good judgment. That's how you learn responsibility, learning how to listen to yourself. Some kids are like, "You think I should go to that party? Because I've got a midterm." It's like, "Keep your ass inside and study. You just answered your question." Learning how to answer your own questions; that's a big part of college.

—ANONYMOUS
BROWN UNIVERSITY, SOPHOMORE

• • • • • • • •

DON'T MISS ANY CLASS, even if you think what the teacher is doing that day isn't significant. You never know what they could say that might affect the school year.

—K.M.
HOWARD UNIVERSITY, SOPHOMORE

• • • • • • • •

FIRST SEMESTER IS KEY; this is what you need to prepare for. From there it is downhill. Get ready to work really hard and then establish a foundation. From there you will be able to just maintain. To do well you have to work hard and the time to begin is freshman year, first semester. So, enjoy your summer and come ready to work hard.

—INSU CHANG
CARNEGIE MELLON UNIVERSITY, JUNIOR

GET YOUR OWN COMPUTER; do not rely on the school's computing facilities. I suggest getting a laptop, and I also suggest getting a laptop lock. I've heard stories where people get up from their computer for a minute—to go to the bathroom or get a drink—and a minute later their computer is stolen.

—*DIANA SHU*
UNIVERSITY OF CALIFORNIA AT BERKELEY, SOPHOMORE

● ● ● ● ● ● ● ●

"Study individually 70% of the time, in groups 20% of the time, and seek the professor's or teaching assistant's help 10% of the time. Divide your time up like this and you're golden."

—*SEAN CAMERON*
PRINCETON UNIVERSITY, SOPHOMORE

● ● ● ● ● ● ● ●

FRESHMAN YEAR IS A CRITICAL TIME to motivate yourself academically. Talk to your academic counselor. If you mess up in your first year, you get in a psychological track and will continue to spiral down. Then your self-esteem goes down and everything else breaks down. Then you drop out.

—*M.N.M.*
COLLEGE OF SAN MATEO, SENIOR

WORK AS HARD AS YOU CAN while keeping yourself sane. College isn't one big party; you've got to understand that you're there to learn and you'll be rewarded for your effort.

—*SEAN CAMERON*
PRINCETON UNIVERSITY, SOPHOMORE

• • • • • • • •

❝❝Set aside a time every day when you study. No matter what else you do that day, when that time comes, you sit down and study. It can be 45 minutes to an hour. If you do it every day, you'll do better in school.❞❞

—*JAKE MALAWAY*
UNIVERSITY OF ILLINOIS, 1995

• • • • • • • •

I DIDN'T DO WELL AT ALL IN SCHOOL. I got kicked out several times because I never went to class; I went out and partied. When I got kicked out of school the last time and got out in the real world and realized there was nothing for me, that turned it around for me. Now I tell the guys I used to party with that I'm in grad school, and they say, "You've come a long way."

—*SCOTT P. WALKER*
GEORGIA INSTITUTE OF TECHNOLOGY

GO TO OFFICE HOURS. Professors will tell you what to expect, and what you need to improve. I've gone to office hours and actually had T.A.'s change my grade because they re-read the paper and they realized that they graded it too harshly. I had it happen twice. I showed them that I did know the material, even if it didn't come out in the paper.

—*EVELIN OCAMPO*
UNIVERSITY OF CALIFORNIA AT SANTA BARBARA, JUNIOR

FRESHMAN FACTOID

Ready for some serious competition? Use this as an incentive to hit the books.

- Forty-two percent of 2003 college-bound high school seniors reported grade averages of A+, A, or A-. Ten years ago, the figure was just 32 percent.
- This year's average grade-point average was 3.29, compared with an average GPA of 3.14 in 1993.
- The average SAT math score—519—is at its highest level in more than 35 years.
- The average SAT verbal score—507—is at its highest level since 1987.
- More students took the SAT—1.4 million, to be more or less exact—in 2002-03 than ever before.

FLIRT WITH THE PROFESSORS. It comes in handy when you need to be late on your term paper because you partied all weekend.

—*ANONYMOUS*
UNIVERSITY OF GEORGIA, 1996

Get some friends who can edit a paper. They'll come in handy. And for every hour you study, do 15 minutes of fun stuff. It helps keep a balance.

—*Conor McNeil*
Emory University
Sophomore

College isn't like high school, you have to actually try to get good grades. When I was a freshman I would write a paper with no thesis and think that I would still get an A on it (which happened in high school). Then you get the paper back and you get a B-minus and it says, "You don't have a thesis." It's hard to slip things by professors; they know the tricks, especially in freshman classes. You have to try that extra bit harder.

—*Kim Kaplan*
Stanford University, Senior

. . . .

Do homework right after class. Study for a test the whole night before. Other students will understand why you look like hell.

—*Richard*
Georgia Southern University, 1992

. . . .

Put in your time in classes first, then bother with clubs and other activities after.

—*Brandon Hogan*
Howard University, Senior

. . . .

Don't wait to write extremely long papers until the night before they're due. Writing under pressure is one thing; writing under extreme, debilitating pressure is something else entirely.

—*Danielle Friedman*
Duke University, Senior

. . . .

I'm an overachiever, so I spent too much time studying my freshman year. My main advice is to make sure you balance studying with having fun. When you have fun, it's a lot easier to sit down and study.

—*Kirsten Gibbs*
Georgia Institute of Technology, Junior

I HAVE TO DO MY WORK RIGHT when it's assigned, otherwise I can't do it.

—*JENNIFER A. SICKLICK*
GEORGE WASHINGTON UNIVERSITY, FRESHMAN

KNOW HOW TO ACCESS ALL the teachers' information. Most professors expect you to be able to download syllabi, assignments, labs, things to write up. Your grades are online. It's more difficult if you can't do these things. It's not impossible, but it's more difficult.

You need to study as much as you can during the day, between classes, rather than wait until the evening when it's more distracting, with TV and friends and social things.

—*LEAH PRICE*
GEORGETOWN UNIVERSITY, SOPHOMORE

• • • • • • • •

BUCKLE DOWN EARLY. Do your work early. The temptation gets greater the later in the year it gets.

—*LAURA GZYZEWSKI*
DESALES UNIVERSITY, JUNIOR

THE KEY TO SURVIVING AND HAVING FREE TIME is to know what the teacher wants you to know and just study that. Skip everything else if it's not necessary to get a good grade in the course.

—*ANONYMOUS*
UNITED STATES MILITARY ACADEMY AT WEST POINT,
JUNIOR

• • • • • • • •

NEVER EVER, GO TO THE LIBRARY ON SATURDAY, unless it's during finals. Take a break one day a week and have fun.

—*STEVE DAVIS*
FLORIDA STATE UNIVERSITY, 1988

An hour of class is worth more than five hours of poring over notes.

—*DAN*
MIAMI UNIVERSITY,
FRESHMAN

IN COLLEGE, YOU HAVE these one- and two-hour chunks in the day with nothing to do. A lot of people spend that time taking a nap or watching TV or checking email or putzing around. It's a good habit to keep a homework assignment on hand, so when you have a spare moment you can pull it out and start reading it. It helps you keep up with it all.

—*CATE*
BROWN UNIVERSITY, JUNIOR

⸻⸻⸻⸻⸻

❝I study about three or four hours every night. For tests, you really can't cram it in, but I do about six hours before tests.❞

—*R.J.*
UNIVERSITY OF DELAWARE, SOPHOMORE

⸻⸻⸻⸻⸻

I STUDY AT NIGHT WHEN IT'S QUIETER; 10 p.m. to 4 a.m. Then I sleep all day. My roommate studies then, too. It's hard to find people you get along with who have the same patterns of sleep.

—*WALTER*
UNIVERSITY OF MARYLAND COLLEGE PARK, SOPHOMORE

⸻⸻⸻⸻⸻

IF YOU GET A B OR A C, DON'T WORRY. When you're going into the job world after graduating, there's no company that's going to say, "Well, you didn't do well in Western Civilization."

—*RHIANNON GULICK*
GEORGETOWN UNIVERSITY, SENIOR

FOR ALL-NIGHTERS, I get a liter of Diet Coke. I've heard of some people who snort Ritalin and Coke. But I wouldn't recommend it. I haven't done that.

> —ANONYMOUS
> YALE UNIVERSITY, SOPHOMORE

• • • • • • • •

✓ **DON'T TAKE ON TOO MUCH AT ONCE.** You can handle a lot, but it's better to not jump into everything and suddenly realize you can't handle it all.

> —CATHERINE G. BARRETT
> BRYN MAWR COLLEGE, SOPHOMORE

• • • • • • • •

YOU CAN'T PROCRASTINATE as much as you do in high school. You get behind, and you get behind, and you get behind, and then you get further and further behind, and you don't know what to do about it. I had a 4.0 in high school, when I could have slept through every class, and now I'm struggling. I have to pick up my study habits.

> —KEVIN BUSHEY
> GEORGIA STATE UNIVERSITY, FRESHMAN

• • • • • • • •

MOUNTAIN DEW AND CAFFEINE PILLS HELP you get through all-nighters.

> —ANONYMOUS
> UNIVERSITY OF RHODE ISLAND, SOPHOMORE

• • • • • • • •

THIS IS SOMETHING MY DAD TOLD ME: You should look at college like a nine-to-five job. You wake up and you do all your work nine to five so that you're not stuck doing your work at 3 a.m., like I always am. Then you're tired and you end up sleeping through your first class, like I always do. So, get your work done early and then you have time to socialize.

> —JENNA
> BOSTON COLLEGE, FRESHMAN

Be careful when buying used books. The person who had the highlighter before you may have been an idiot.

—J.T.
UNIVERSITY OF FLORIDA, 1990

GO OUT TO PARTY ON THURSDAYS, Fridays and Saturdays, but stay at home on the other days. I don't have classes on Friday; you should try to schedule that. And I don't study on Sundays; that's for watching football. During the week, I go to class and then study about two hours a night.

—*FRED*
UNIVERSITY OF RHODE ISLAND, JUNIOR

• • • • • • • •

SOME OF MY MOST PRODUCTIVE STUDY SESSIONS were studying in groups. Find a classroom that's empty in the evening, write notes and questions on the chalkboard, quiz each other, and have fun with it.

—*K. HARMA*
WESTERN WASHINGTON UNIVERSITY, 2001

• • • • • • • •

DON'T BE A COPYCAT

In a recent survey, 38% of college students said that they had "cut-and-pasted" from the Internet without citing the source. But beware: 20% of the faculty members surveyed said they use computer-based tools to help them identify cases of student plagiarism.

• • • • • • • •

GET INVOLVED WITH PEOPLE who are taking classes with you. When you have friends who are doing the same thing with the same goals, it's easy to work together, and you can build off each other, rather than trying to do everything by yourself.

—*COURTNEY WOLFE*
GEORGIA STATE UNIVERSITY, JUNIOR

TAKE ALL THE INTRODUCTORY COURSES. Don't try to be Superman. You may have taken all A.P. courses in high school, but college is different. Read the textbooks. Drink lots of coffee, too.

> —*ERIC*
> *HUNTER COLLEGE, FRESHMAN*

• • • • • • • •

TEACHERS DON'T EXPLAIN, so it's good to have people help you. I do my work during the week and I give myself the whole weekend to go out.

> —*WHITNEY HIBBARD*
> *GEORGIA INSTITUTE OF TECHNOLOGY, SOPHOMORE*

I HAD TO GET USED TO READING A LOT. For my business class, I have about 40 pages to read after every class. For Latin American studies, there's a chapter for that, too. As soon as I get out of classes I do my homework. Then I do more homework at night.

> —*S.E.*
> *UNIVERSITY OF MARYLAND, FRESHMAN*

• • • • • • • •

IN HIGH SCHOOL, I NEVER REALLY DID ANY WORK during the day. Here, it's essential to do some work during the day because I find myself easily distracted at night. There's so much freedom and you have so much time in your day, it's tough to balance it all.

> —*MOLLY DERINGER*
> *BROWN UNIVERSITY, FRESHMAN*

• • • • • • • •

DON'T STUDY IN YOUR ROOM; you won't ever get to it. Your phone and neighbors will be too enticing. I would suggest a quiet cube at the library, if you really need to get something done.

> —*J.S.*
> *UNIVERSITY OF GEORGIA, 1995*

TIME MANAGEMENT—a lot of the homework is not due, but you still have to get it done. So, I write out a schedule—it's weekly.

—*MANI*
UNIVERSITY OF MARYLAND, FRESHMAN

• • • • • • • •

❝It's good to go to class every day, at least to make an impression that you care.❞

—*LUKE MOUGHON*
GEORGIA INSTITUTE OF TECHNOLOGY, SOPHOMORE

• • • • • • • •

✓ **I DON'T CRAM FOR EXAMS.** I have trouble studying and focusing. I just assume that I know the material. Instead of cramming, I go over the notes I've taken in class and I go over what I highlighted in my book, and by that point, I probably know everything that I need to know. I take good notes; in an hour-and-a-half class, I write four pages. But I don't study until it's time for the test. I just review it. I never pull an all-nighter.

—*EDITH ZIMMERMAN*
WESLEYAN UNIVERSITY, SOPHOMORE

• • • • • • • •

I PULLED AN ALL-NIGHTER LAST NIGHT. I get an adrenaline rush from the fact that it's the last second, and I can stay up late without a problem. But I don't recommend doing it, if you can avoid it.

—*M.M.*
NEW YORK UNIVERSITY, SENIOR

DON'T MISS EVEN ONE DAY of homework. If you fall behind, it's so much harder to catch up.

—*NATASHA PIRZADA*
GEORGETOWN UNIVERSITY, SOPHOMORE

• • • • • • • •

I GO TO SCHOOL IN A BIG CITY, and there's always the temptation to go out and do something. You can't escape it. You have to realize, when night-time comes, you're going to want to go out. So you have to do your work in the day; otherwise, your work won't get done.

—*CATHY*
COLUMBIA UNIVERSITY, SENIOR

• • • • • • • •

BEST LINE FROM A U.S. PRESIDENT AT A COLLEGE GRADUATION CEREMONY

"Congratulations to the class of 2001. To those of you who received honors, awards, and distinctions, I say: Well done. And to the C students. . . *(applause)*. . . I say: You, too, can be President of the United States."

—*GEORGE W. BUSH*
COMMENCEMENT ADDRESS, YALE UNIVERSITY, MAY 21, 2001

• • • • • • • •

I ONCE STAYED UP THREE NIGHTS back to back. It was fairly intense. I drank coffee, but it was mostly adrenaline; you do what you've got to do. Also, I used to eat chocolate-covered espresso beans. They taste good and it gives you a little boost.

—*B.*
MASSACHUSETTS INSTITUTE OF TECHNOLOGY, 1998

THERE'S LESS DAY-TO-DAY WORK than you have in high school, so you think that you don't have that much and you continue not doing that much. Then it hits you. It all piles up. That's not good.

—*LUCY LINDSEY*
HARVARD UNIVERSITY, FRESHMAN

* * * * * * * *

"Get old tests from previous semesters; old tests and note-books. There's a code name for this at most schools; find this out the first week of school."

—*SEBASTIAN*
GEORGIA INSTITUTE OF TECHNOLOGY, 1985

* * * * * * * *

YOU GET ADDICTED TO IM. Don't get addicted. You'll be writing a paper and you think, "I'm bored." So you start chatting on IM and a one-hour paper turns into like five hours. Take your Internet cable and have someone hide it when you're writing your paper, so you don't get distracted.

—*ASHLEY*
GEORGETOWN UNIVERSITY, SOPHOMORE

* * * * * * * *

I'M TAKING BIOLOGY and you have to read every night to keep up. Two or three days before our exam, I decided I would study for the test. I read eight chapters in three days. That's how I studied.

—*PATRICK*
UNIVERSITY OF RHODE ISLAND, FRESHMAN

ONCE, I HAD A CLASS where I was getting lecture notes online and I ended up not going to class for the last month. So I read a month of notes and two weeks of reading the night before the final. And then I found out there was a paper due that I didn't know about. So I wrote a paper the night before the final. I studied from 8 p.m. until 4 a.m. I ended up getting a B in the class.

—*ERIC FRIES*
BOSTON UNIVERSITY, 1997

• • • • • • • •

I PULLED MY FIRST ALL-NIGHTER LAST WEEK. I did two nights in a row. I was up from 5 a.m. on Tuesday morning to 3 p.m. on Thursday afternoon. It was tough. I went to class to turn in my second paper on Thursday; I got there, sat down, and hit the desk. I fell asleep and someone woke me up at the end of class and I turned in my paper. Diet Coke with lemon pulled me through.

—*WHITNEY*
YALE UNIVERSITY, FRESHMAN

• • • • • • • •

DON'T TRY TO STUDY ON A FRIDAY NIGHT. You're trying to study in the dorms and people keep coming in. Don't even try.

—*NOURA BAKKOUR*
GEORGETOWN UNIVERSITY, SENIOR

• • • • • • • •

YOU CAN BALANCE IT. If there's a choice between doing work and going to a party, I would probably go to the party. I would go to the party before I try to do my paper, but you should try to do your paper before you go to the party.

—*SWEETS*
GEORGIA STATE UNIVERSITY, JUNIOR

YOU HAVE TO KEEP WEIRD HOURS. Sometimes at 3 a.m. you're doing your work. But it's just what you have to do.

—*T.O.*
HOWARD UNIVERSITY, SOPHOMORE

• • • • • • • •

ONE OF THE LESS POSITIVE MEMORIES from my freshman year occurred during final exams of first semester. I had stayed up until 4 a.m. studying material for my art history final, and was extremely confident that I would perform well and get the A that I had expected based on my 96 average going into it. I awoke the next morning to the horrifying realization that my alarm clock had not gone off and I had already missed the entire exam. I was so disappointed and angry at myself. The zero score averaged into my grade brought it down to a B-, which brought my G.P.A. down almost half a point. To avoid this disappointment in the future, I make sure to set a backup alarm, and sometimes even a backup-backup alarm, on important test days.

—*MAXWELL HOCKSTAD*
STATE UNIVERSITY OF NEW YORK AT ALBANY, SOPHOMORE

A Minor Crisis? Choosing a Major

OK, now you're in college. Like most freshmen, you probably have no idea what you want to do with your life, so how can you choose a major? When do you need to worry about it? Are you doomed if you choose the wrong one? What happens if you just can't commit? Read on . . .

DO NOT WASTE YOUR TIME—that is your most valuable commodity in life. If what you're doing no longer interests you, stop and re-evaluate it. Don't pursue a degree that doesn't matter to you anymore. You don't want to get halfway into your life doing something that you hate. Ultimately, your happiness is what counts.

—*LINDSAY PETSCH*
GEORGIA STATE UNIVERSITY, JUNIOR

IT'S SCARY TO CHASE YOUR DREAMS IN COLLEGE.

—*ADAM PENA*
AMERICAN REPERTORY THEATER AT HARVARD JUNIOR

I'm taking a variety of classes before I declare my major. I recommend that, especially if you're unsure about what you want to do.

—H.P.
University of Pennsylvania Freshman

TALKING TO SENIORS IS A GOOD WAY to help you decide on your major. I didn't know any seniors when I was a freshman, but it would have been nice. Sophomore year I talked to seniors who told me what kinds of jobs they were getting, who was getting hired and who wasn't, and who was getting the kinds of jobs they wanted and who was having to settle. That was useful.

—*Katharine*
Stanford University, Junior

• • • • • • • •

FIGURE OUT YOUR MAJOR EARLY ON, as opposed to busily trying to satisfy all of your college require-ments. Often, some of the classes that fall in your major curriculum of studies double as the core required classes.

—*Diana Shu*
University of California at Berkeley, Sophomore

• • • • • • • •

I STARTED OFF AS A FINE-ARTS MAJOR. After one semester I switched to advertising. The fine-arts classes were filled only by women and gay men, and lots of cool guys took advertising classes. After attending an all-girls high school I wanted to see some hunky men. I ended up changing my major a total of seven times and ended up getting a degree in history. I should have just stuck to fine arts, which is what I really loved and wanted to do.

—*Lynn Lamousin*
Louisiana State University, 1988

• • • • • • • •

TAKE A VARIETY OF COURSES. Something inside tells you where to go and you need to follow that feeling. If you don't follow that feeling, you're going to run into some real trouble.

—*Phillip N. Albertson*
University of Wisconsin—Stevens Point, 1996

IF YOU'RE LOOKING FOR A GREAT MAJOR, find out what the school's athletes are majoring in. They are usually concentrated in just a few majors or departments. This does not automatically mean these are the easy majors; often they have low student-teacher ratios, individualized attention, and more flexibility for students who go out of town for games or competitions.

—*WENDY W.*
UNIVERSITY OF GEORGIA, 1996

• • • • • • • •

LIFE IS WAY TOO SHORT TO STUDY something you really do not want to do. I used to be a psychology major with a theater minor. I remember talking to a friend who asked me what I really wanted to do. My response was that I wanted to be an actress and move to New York. He said, "Then why are you a psychology major?" I said, "Well, just in case, I'll have a back-up." But it seemed as though I was already setting myself up to fail. So I switched majors and graduated with a B.A. in theater with honors. Now I live in New York, beginning the journey I have always wanted to take.

—*LESLIE M.*
UNIVERSITY OF FLORIDA, 1995

• • • • • • • •

MY SCHOOL ALLOWS YOU TO CREATE YOUR MAJOR, which is inspiring, but you need a lot of persistence to make it happen—there's no blueprint in forging your own path. I want to major in advertising, so I'm running around, talking to my counselor, meeting with teachers to see which classes are appropriate, and working with administrators to get clearance. The payoff is that one day I'll have the same job as Mel Gibson in *What Women Want!*

—*COLE RYAN*
SONOMA STATE UNIVERSITY, SOPHOMORE

DON'T DETERMINE YOUR MAJOR TOO SOON. I'm in finance and I don't know why. Keep your mind open. Undergraduate isn't what determines your future now; it's graduate school.

—*M.A.A.*
GEORGE WASHINGTON UNIVERSITY, SENIOR

• • • • • • • •

"If you have no clue, take the time to try everything. I picked math because it's the easiest for me. It wasn't a wise decision because I don't have much interest in it. But I felt a lot of pressure when it came time to pick a major, and there's no turning back now."

—*SUSAN LIPPERT*
EMORY UNIVERSITY, JUNIOR

• • • • • • • •

STUDY DIFFERENT THINGS. You can't make a decision on your major if you don't know anything about different fields. Even if it's just picking up a book and reading something, you'll have a better understanding of what you like or don't like. And study something you like. You might think, well, that makes money, but then when you do it, you feel like it's work. Do something that's fun.

—*K.M.*
HOWARD UNIVERSITY, SOPHOMORE

KNOW WHAT YOU *DON'T* WANT

I went to college with absolutely no knowledge of what types of careers were available out there. My parents were in the restaurant business (I definitely didn't want to do that) and they dealt a lot with bankers and accountants. I honestly thought I had to be a banker or accountant. I ended up as a finance major. After graduation I asked a friend of mine why he chose environmental engineering and his answer was that he really wanted a job that would allow him to be outside rather than confined to an office. I wish I had thought of something like that. Now that I've been in the work force for 15 years and have seen all of the different and varied job opportunities there are, I wish I had spent  more time thinking and learning about potential career paths and vocations before selecting a major. You're much more likely to find a career you truly enjoy if you have more opportunities to select from.

—R.D.W.
UNIVERSITY OF VIRGINIA, 1988

GET TO KNOW THE GRAD STUDENTS. They know what's going on with the department, often more than the professors do. And lots of classes are taught by grad students, so that helps you.

I had a total lack of advising. I had one appointment with a generic advisor. I was assigned someone who didn't know anything about my major, which was archaeology. The guy told me he knew nothing about that, and he couldn't help me with my major. After that, the only time I had contact with the advising department was to fix things they screwed up.
—*ERIC FRIES*
BOSTON UNIVERSITY, 1997

• • • • • • • •

THIS COLLEGE TAKES THE CAKE

Kansas State University claims to be the only place you can get college-level degrees in baking science, feed science, or milling science and management—degrees which, according to the school, "prepare you for a rewarding career in the grain processing and utilizing industries."

• • • • • • • •

I WANTED TO BE AN ACTOR. I'm from a working-class family and they don't know anything about the arts, and they were scared. They were like, "Get some kind of degree that will pay and then you can do the acting for fun." But I said, "No." I was scared too, because I didn't know a whole lot about it. But I found there is work out there, and I really enjoy what I do now.
—*ADAM PENA*
AMERICAN REPERTORY THEATER AT HARVARD, JUNIOR

DECIDE ON A MAJOR YOUR FRESHMAN YEAR. I ended up going to school for nearly five years because I couldn't pick a major. If I had been more decisive from the start, I would have accomplished my goal in a much timelier fashion. Take advantage of your student center's counseling service. Sometimes they will offer Career Inventory and Personality Exams for free to help you figure out what you want to do.

—*J.S.*
UNIVERSITY OF GEORGIA, 1995

• • • • • • • •

TAKE AS WIDE A RANGE OF CLASSES as possible your freshman year. Don't feel pressured to choose a major or to take all classes specific to your major, unless you are absolutely certain it is a career you want to pursue.

I was pressured by guidance counselors, family members, and my own school to choose a major before starting my freshman year. So, while most of my friends took general education classes to expose themselves to as many career options as possible, I took more difficult classes, very specific to my major, that would later affect my G.P.A. within my major. Harder classes, coupled with the adjustment to the college "lifestyle" and a part-time job, left me strapped for time; as a result, my G.P.A. suffered greatly. After my first semester I changed to Undeclared, took classes from five different departments, and will now graduate with a degree in two different majors.

—*COREY CARVALHO*
UNIVERSITY OF MASSACHUSETTS AT AMHERST, SENIOR

TAKE YOUR ADVISOR SERIOUSLY. They can really help you avoid academic minefields and learn the lay of the land. You don't need to keep the advisor they give you. If you like your assigned advisor, great. If not, try and find another professor who you like, and switch. You can change your major, so even if you're forced to choose one before starting college, don't feel locked in. And don't feel that you need to begin your major obligations right away. Choose some classes that you're really interested in, even if they have nothing to do with your major.

—*ANONYMOUS*
UNION COLLEGE

• • • • • • • •

DON'T GO WITH SOMETHING YOU'RE GOOD AT. Go with what you like. I know people who applied for schools in something they knew they were good at, and once they got in they realized they didn't really want to do it, but they feel stuck. The real waste of money is when you get a degree that you don't really want.

—*ERIC MCINTOSH*
UNIVERSITY OF NORTH CAROLINA AT CHAPEL HILL, JUNIOR

Food For Thought: Pop-Tarts, Beer, and Other Essential Nutrients

You've probably been warned about college food and about the notorious Freshman 15. Until they figure out a way to Fedex your meals from home, you're going to have to make do with college food. Don't worry—most people survive it.

TAKE EVERY FREE MEAL THAT YOU CAN GET.
Generally, the dining hall is not bad. But when you eat it seven days a week, it gets pretty old, no matter how good the food is. Every time someone wants to take you out, take them up on it. If nothing else, it's a good way to make friends or meet people.

—JONATHAN COHEN
EMORY UNIVERSITY, SENIOR

DON'T EAT THE FOOD.
—SIERRA
CAL POLY SAN LUIS OBISPO, JUNIOR

THE FIRST INCLINATION WHEN YOU GET TO COLLEGE is to eat anything you want. Mom isn't there making sure you eat your vegetables. But three months and 15 pounds later you find out why a mom is a good thing when it comes to food.

—*D.R.*
UNIVERSITY OF NORTH CAROLINA, 1991

• • • • • • • •

Freshman 15 really exists. Freshman 50, sometimes.

—*H.P.*
UNIVERSITY OF PENNSYLVANIA FRESHMAN

I RECOMMEND THAT ONE ACQUIRE a taste for hummus. Hummus can really be put onto anything, it comes in all sorts of flavors, it's healthy, and it's relatively cheap if bought in bulk. Seriously, try and think of something that hummus wouldn't be good on; you can't!

—*STEVEN COY*
SAN DIEGO STATE UNIVERSITY, SOPHOMORE

• • • • • • • •

DON'T THINK THAT YOU WON'T GAIN that Freshman 15 by ordering pizza while watching late-night TV (in my case, David Letterman), eating Burger King, and drinking every night.

—*K.E.R.*
FLORIDA STATE UNIVERSITY, 1997

• • • • • • • •

DON'T BUY THE FULL MEAL TICKET, unless you're sure you can eat breakfast every day. I made it to breakfast once the whole year. When I got up, I didn't have time to go downstairs and eat; I had to go to class.

—*JAKE MALAWAY*
UNIVERSITY OF ILLINOIS, 1995

• • • • • • • •

I WOULDN'T GET ON ANY MEAL PLAN. I would fend for myself, food-wise. Cafeteria food is bad.

—*ERICA MARIOLA*
EMORY UNIVERSITY, 2002

BE CAREFUL WHAT YOU COOK in your toaster. My friend bought some frozen hot dogs—like, six of them—and then one day she was hungry so she tried to cook them in the toaster in her dorm room, and smoke came out of it and she set off the fire alarm. So she had to go to peer review, which was funny because most of the cases they get in peer review are people using excessive bandwidth from downloading too much, and then they get this interesting case. For punishment they said she had to make a few posters saying, "Be safe—don't put hot dogs in toasters."

—*J.R. MCKINNEY*
UNIVERSITY OF CALIFORNIA AT BERKELEY, SOPHOMORE

• • • • • • • •

THE HOT-DOG VENDOR will become your new best friend.

—*J.G.*
FLORIDA STATE UNIVERSITY, 1991

• • • • • • • •

ONE TIME MY FRIEND AND I SPLIT A SANDWICH—a ham and cheese and lettuce and tomato sandwich. They make it in front of you, and the lady cut it in half. Right when I was going to eat my half, I saw a dead fly-half, sticking out where she had cut it. My friend was taking a bite so I had to tell her, "Stop eating it, stop eating it!" We were so grossed out. We were like, "We're never going to eat here ever again." And they didn't refund us, either. They couldn't give us back our money because of how the registers work. They said, "We'll make you a new one," but we were like, "No." After that we tried to eat off campus as much as possible. It was nasty.

—*MARY LE*
SANTA CLARA UNIVERSITY, JUNIOR

BEST THINGS TO COOK UP IN A DORM KITCHEN

Brownies (from a mix)

Instant noodle-and-sauce packages

Pasta and sauce in a jar

Precooked chicken meat

Store-bought cookie dough

Whatever the recommended meal plan is—always order less. Cafeteria food sucks!

—*ARIELLA*
UNIVERSITY OF
PENNSYLVANIA
SENIOR

BUY LOTS OF TUPPERWARE CONTAINERS to take to the cafeteria and sneak food out, so you don't have to buy it. You're paying for a meal plan anyway.

> —*MEG*
> *UNIVERSITY OF NORTH CAROLINA, 2001*

• • • • • • • •

GET YOUR OWN MINI-FRIDGE and buy your own food. Buy Easy Mac—it's microwaveable macaroni and cheese—so you don't need a stove.

> —*SIERRA*
> *CAL POLY SAN LUIS OBISPO, JUNIOR*

• • • • • • • •

DON'T EAT THE EGGS IN THE DINING COMMONS— they're fake. Anything you can eat from a bowl, like cereal and salad, is good. Don't eat a lot of fast food just because it's there and it's cheap. Jamba Juice is the way to go: it won't make you fat, it's kind of healthy, and it doesn't smell bad so you can take it to class and no one will yell at you. You get these people who go to class with a burger and onion rings and sit there for an hour in class and it's gross.

> —*KYM*
> *SAN JOSE STATE UNIVERSITY, SOPHOMORE*

• • • • • • • •

THE FRESHMAN 15 HAPPENS TO EVERYONE, and don't believe anyone who tells you otherwise. I guess I learned the hard way, but just because you can take as much as you want in a dining hall does not mean you should. Dining-hall coffee leaves a lot to be desired, but it is sometimes the only thing that can keep you awake after pulling an all-nighter. Milk, sugar, repeat, and the stuff can become somewhat consumable.

> —*AMY*
> *PRINCETON UNIVERSITY, FRESHMAN*

I HAVE A LOT OF SNACKS IN MY ROOM—macaroni and cheese and peanut butter and jelly. You might want to bring that kind of stuff, in case you can't make it to the cafeteria or don't want to go, for whatever reason.

—*ANONYMOUS*
UNIVERSITY OF MARYLAND, FRESHMAN

• • • • • • • •

"You're going to gain weight and you're going to take it off the next summer. Don't worry about it. Buy some fat pants. Everybody I know gained a lot of weight."

—*HANNAH*
EMORY UNIVERSITY, JUNIOR

• • • • • • • •

A STORE NEAR OUR COLLEGE SELLS what they call Tanks—it's a half-gallon of iced coffee for two dollars. It's awesome.

—*CHRISTINE*
UNIVERSITY OF RHODE ISLAND, SOPHOMORE

• • • • • • • •

I HAVE WEIRD EATING HABITS. I eat rice cakes and dried pineapple. I don't know why. Also, chocolate helps.

—*ANONYMOUS*
YALE UNIVERSITY, SOPHOMORE

The dining hall was good. But I'm glad I don't eat there anymore.

—*CHRIS MCANDREW*
UNIVERSITY OF DELAWARE, JUNIOR

I LIVED ON COFFEE. If I hadn't had coffee last year, I would have died.

—*ANONYMOUS*
UNIVERSITY OF VIRGINIA, SOPHOMORE

• • • • • • • •

WATCH OUT FOR THE BUFFET and make sure to exercise, because the Freshman 15 is a very real phenomenon.

—*RUTH FEINBLUM*
BRYN MAWR COLLEGE, JUNIOR

Don't be fooled by the Freshman 15. Real men go for the Freshman 30; at least that's how I cope with it.

—*ADAM*
  ELON UNIVERSITY,
  SOPHOMORE

THIS IS THE FOOD HERE: They have all the basic food, and then they have these huge vats of sauce. And they just slosh the sauce over the food and it becomes disgusting.

—*LUCY LINDSEY*
HARVARD UNIVERSITY, FRESHMAN

• • • • • • • •

SCARF THAT FOOD DOWN! Everyone eats faster than you. I had to go to the cafeteria 15 minutes before my roommates and friends just to be finished at the same time.

—*JOY HEARNDON*
MICHIGAN TECHNOLOGICAL
UNIVERSITY, 2002

• • • • • • • •

MOST IMPORTANT PIECE OF ADVICE I ever received about college food: If you find a hair in your food in the dining hall, just assume it's yours and move on.

—*MATT LACKNER*
PRINCETON UNIVERSITY, 2002

• • • • • • • •

FIND RESTAURANTS THAT HAVE BUFFETS; you can eat all you want.

—*S.E.*
UNIVERSITY OF MARYLAND, FRESHMAN

Money for Your Life: Working and Finances

*W*ell, somebody's got to pay for it all. Maybe you've got a nice, fat, trust fund, but most likely you're getting by with a combination of family help, loans, and luck, not to mention a job. How can you balance all you want to do in these four years with those incessant demands on your bank account? Those who have gone before you have some suggestions.

DON'T GET ALL THE BILLS IN YOUR NAME. When I lived off campus, the bills were all in my name, which was really stupid. I had problems with my roommates, and even though they eventually paid me back, they would take forever. I had to sit there wondering if they were ever going to pay me.

—*MARY-CLAIRE CONBOY*
UNIVERSITY OF CALIFORNIA AT SANTA CRUZ, SENIOR

IT'S A GOOD EXPERIENCE TO HAVE A JOB.

—*M.B.*
SAN JOSE STATE UNIVERSITY, 2002

I THINK IT'S GOOD TO WORK A FEW HOURS a week at least, and that can be your weekend spending money. I worked at a restaurant and I used my tips as my spending money. It's also a good way to meet people in your school's town, so you get away from college, so you can vent, so you can be well rounded.

—*MEGHAN*
UNIVERSITY OF NOTRE DAME, JUNIOR

• • • • • • • •

Work while in school. It helps you avoid debt and gives you some financial independence.

—*P.O.*
MOORHEAD STATE UNIVERSITY, 1993

I REFEREED FOR INTRAMURALS. I was lucky, because my parents helped me out quite a bit. But even if you do get help or are on scholarship, I would recommend getting a job at some point. I know some people who work at the library, and they just sit there and study while getting paid for it. On the other hand, I knew people who did research for work in college, and that was like adding another three- or six-hour class; that was tough.

—*JOHN BENTLEY*
TRINITY UNIVERSITY, 1995

• • • • • • • •

THERE ARE A LOT OF GOOD BUDGETING PROGRAMS for your computer; that's what helped me. You have to stay on top of it. Come up with a system for tracking your bank account or you will get screwed. Those charges will add up.

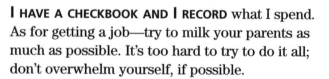

—*RUTH FEINBLUM*
BRYN MAWR COLLEGE, JUNIOR

• • • • • • • •

I HAVE A CHECKBOOK AND I RECORD what I spend. As for getting a job—try to milk your parents as much as possible. It's too hard to try to do it all; don't overwhelm yourself, if possible.

—*JESSICA*
BARNARD COLLEGE, JUNIOR

IT'S BETTER NOT TO WORK your freshman year, or at least the first quarter, because you're still adjusting. I was overwhelmed by the homework. And if you work your first year you don't get to meet as many people. But later, working helps to keep you focused. You gain skills and it helps you learn to budget your time. It's good to work on campus because they're flexible, and they'll give you time off during finals.

—*ABBY HERNANDEZ*
UNIVERSITY OF CALIFORNIA AT SANTA BARBARA, JUNIOR

· · · · · · · ·

I WORK AS A WAITRESS ON CAMPUS. I work 11:30 a.m.–2:30 p.m. so it fits well into my work/study plan. My nights are open, I'm paid in cash, and I get tips. I keep a car at school, which is an expense, so I enjoy working; it's empowering. My parents are generous, but again, I enjoy having my own income and have been able to save a lot, which is important to me as I plan for my future.

—*VANESSA VALENZUELA*
SONOMA STATE UNIVERSITY, SOPHOMORE

· · · · · · · ·

IF I WERE WRITING A BOOK about the things they don't tell you when you enter college, the first chapter would cover the hidden costs of living away from home—travel, long distance telephone, and school supplies, for example.

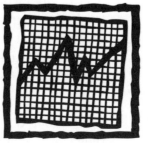

However, the most shocking expense is food: the midnight pizzas, the birthday dinners, the celebration dinners, and the random exoduses from campus when you just can't take it anymore, add up in a hurry.

—*ADAM*
ELON UNIVERSITY, SOPHOMORE

If you're a girl, you usually don't have to buy alcohol. Guys buy it for you. That's a big money-saver.

—*ANONYMOUS*
YALE UNIVERSITY
SOPHOMORE

I HAVE AN ON-CAMPUS JOB in the women's studies department and in the dance department. Also, they have a bartending agency here and you get paid $20 an hour. I took the course so I can do that when I want to. I don't think all colleges have a bartending course, but usually there's a babysitting agency. Working on campus doesn't pay as much, but it's so much easier. There's nothing to do; I get paid for doing my homework.

—*LAUREN WEBSTER*
BARNARD COLLEGE, JUNIOR

• • • • • • • •

"Start thinking about how you're spending your money. It's really easy to start spending a lot."

—*MOLLY DERINGER*
BROWN UNIVERSITY, FRESHMAN

• • • • • • • •

DON'T THINK THAT WHEN YOU GO to the ATM machine and do a "current balance" check, the figure it spits out is really your current balance. I thought it was. I amassed probably $500 in bounced check fees my first semester. No one ever taught me how to balance a checkbook. Get your parents to teach you that before you go, and then make sure you do it when you're at school.

And don't sign up for every student credit card you're offered in the mail. I did, and got into what they call "credit trouble."

—*K.E.R.*
FLORIDA STATE UNIVERSITY, 1997

GET THE FLOOD INSURANCE

In January of my freshman year I was woken up one cold morning at three o'clock by the fire alarm going off in the hall of my dorm. I ran outside as fast as I could in my pajama shorts and t-shirt. They turned off the fire alarm, but something in the sprinkler system had malfunctioned, setting off the sprinkler in our hall, so we had a good five inches of disgusting, rusty water on the floors of our rooms. I had stored all of my schoolbooks under my bed, and they were now completely submerged in water, along with a good deal of dirty clothes strewn about, my printer, and all the electronics. The  school informed me that because I hadn't bought insurance through them, they wouldn't cover any of the damage.

So keep your room neat, because you never know when you'll have gallons of rusty water flooding your room. And if the school offers insurance for a reasonable price, it's worth getting.

—MOLLY DONAHUE
SYRACUSE UNIVERSITY, SOPHOMORE

IT'S HARD TO JUGGLE SCHOOL AND WORK. If you're not getting an allowance from home, it's very hard. My mom is barely middle class, and because of that, I'm definitely part of the minority here.
—*KEISHA*
EMORY UNIVERSITY, SENIOR

• • • • • • • •

GET SOME FIRSTHAND OFFICE EXPERIENCE before you graduate. You learn how to interact with people, and you have your own money for the first time in your life. You can pay for tuition and rent; you can live on your own. That freedom can help you achieve more.
—*M.B.*
SAN JOSE STATE UNIVERSITY, 2002

• • • • • • • •

FRESHMAN FACTOID

How students cover the cost of college:

• Financial aid and scholarships (37%)

• Pay for it themselves (9%)

• Parents pay (13%)

• Some combination of the above (41%)

I TRY NOT TO GO OUT too much or go shopping too much and just try to keep the costs down any way I can.
—*CHANA WEINER*
BARNARD COLLEGE, SOPHOMORE

• • • • • • • •

GET A CHECK CARD INSTEAD OF A CREDIT CARD. But be careful with it. And don't use the on-campus bank—it's always the worst bank.
—*ANONYMOUS*
JOHNS HOPKINS UNIVERSITY, JUNIOR

• • • • • • • •

EVERY TIME YOU GO OUT, when all your friends are having that last drink, cut yourself off; don't have that last drink. Then, go home and put the money you saved in a piggy bank. You'll be surprised how quickly it adds up. And you can go out and buy a new outfit.
—*S.G.*
COLUMBIA UNIVERSITY, SENIOR

12

Fashion and (eventually) Laundry

*U*nless you're enrolled in the state penitentiary or a monastery, where the dress code is decided for you, you'll probably have to make some tough decisions about what to wear around campus. Here are some tips on dressing up and dressing down, along with some lessons on keeping you—and your threads—lemon-fresh.

IF YOU LIVE IN A DORM AND YOUR BATHROOM is down the hall, get good shower shoes. If you go barefoot, by mid-October they'll be studying the stuff on your feet in biology class.

—*J.T.*
UNIVERSITY OF FLORIDA, 1990

• • • • • • • •

I GO HOME TO DO LAUNDRY.

—*CAITLIN LOCKE*
UNIVERSITY OF DELAWARE, FRESHMAN

ALWAYS DRESS A CUT ABOVE THE REST. COLLEGE HAS A LOT TO DO WITH IMAGE.

—*SEAN CAMERON*
PRINCETON UNIVERSITY SOPHOMORE

DO NOT BRING CLOTHES that require ironing or dry cleaning or special handling. And do not loan your favorite shirt to a party-happy friend if you want it back in the same condition. If you are female, leave your handbag at home. No one brings a purse to a party, and during the day your backpack is your bag.

—*J.*
UNIVERSITY OF GEORGIA, 1996

. . . .

" No one will really notice if you wear the same two or three (or one) pair of jeans or khakis— it's the shirt that people notice. So get plenty of shirts and one or two pairs of jeans and you can cut laundry efforts in half. "

—*DAN*
MIAMI UNIVERSITY, FRESHMAN

. . . .

GUYS, BRING KHAKIS in the fall and then cut them off in the spring.

—*STEVE DAVIS*
FLORIDA STATE UNIVERSITY, 1988

. . . .

BUY A STURDY, ROOMY BACKPACK. You'll need it to hold thick, heavy textbooks for courses like English, political science, biology, algebra, etc.

—*BRIAN TURNER*
UNIVERSITY OF GEORGIA, 1996

SPECIAL HYGIENE SECTION

Thanks to all those imperfectly socialized freshmen who made this page possible—and necessary.

If possible, try to find the shower in your dorm with the best pressure and the most considerate bathroom users and ask politely to share it with them. A nice hot shower under a showerhead with good pressure is a great way to unwind. Be considerate of other bathroom users! Don't leave a mess for your janitors; they are there to maintain a standard of hygiene, not to clean up your messes.

> —*Ariel Melendez*
> *Princeton University, Freshman*

• • • • • • • •

Just because you can't smell it, doesn't mean it's not there. Shower at least once a day and especially after coming from the gym.

> —*Khalil Sullivan*
> *Princeton University, Junior*

• • • • • • • •

Showering every day is a must. There are college students who think they can go more than a day without showering, but they are sorely mistaken. Trust me when I say that it can be painfully (and nauseatingly) obvious when someone has not bathed properly. As a courtesy to those around you, remember to take a shower.

> —*Joshua Berkov*
> *Brown University, Junior*

• • • • • • • •

Even if it doesn't bother you to walk around for a few days without a shower—please, oh God, before you forgo the morning cleaning, please think of the person sitting next to you in class.

> —*Adam*
> *Elon University, Sophomore*

RESIST CONFORMITY. We have too many Gap kids and Abercrombie lookalikes running around campus.

—*KHALIL SULLIVAN*
PRINCETON UNIVERSITY, JUNIOR

• • • • • • • •

NEVER ATTEND A PUNK-ROCK CONCERT in a sundress and Keds sneakers. I left a Ramones concert wearing only one shoe after getting caught in the middle of a group of overeager slam-dancers. Doc Martens would have been a better choice.

—*LYNN LAMOUSIN*
LOUISIANA STATE UNIVERSITY, 1988

• • • • • • • •

IF YOU FIND YOURSELF IN THE LAUNDRY ROOM and don't know how to wash your own clothes, do not push the "help" button. This button is for security purposes only; for example, if you are attacked. No little helper will come and help you wash your clothes. Instead, you will sound the alarm and call the police.

—*ANONYMOUS*
UNIVERSITY OF PENNSYLVANIA, SENIOR

• • • • • • • •

IF YOU WANT TO BE COOL, don't wear anything with your school name or colors on it. It's called Freshman Fashion Wear for a reason.

—*J.G.*
FLORIDA STATE UNIVERSITY, 1991

• • • • • • • •

I HAVE NOT USED MY COMB YET. I have not worn any college shirts, either. A lot of the kids do that, but I haven't worn one, and my mom packed 15 of them.

—*BAYLESS PARSLEY*
UNIVERSITY OF VIRGINIA, FRESHMAN

You can wear your pajamas around campus; you won't be the only one.

—*AMY FORBES*
MISSISSIPPI STATE UNIVERSITY, 2003

WARNING: DON'T WASH DOWN COMFORTERS. You'll
flood the laundry room and ruin your blanket.

—*ETHAN WASSERMAN*
BOSTON UNIVERSITY, JUNIOR

• • • • • • • •

" During crunch time, you need
only a few pieces of clothing:
Sweatpants in school color of
choice, comfy tank top or ratty
T-shirt, and a hoodie. "

—*AMY*
PRINCETON UNIVERSITY, FRESHMAN

• • • • • • • •

MY FRESHMAN-YEAR ROOMMATE and I were polar
opposites. She was a city girl from D.C., really
stylish, and she hated the way I dressed. When I
would get up in the morning to go to class, I would
throw on my jeans, a sweatshirt, and my
Birkenstocks, and for the first couple of weeks she
would block the door so I couldn't leave. She would
say, "Uh-uh, girl. You are not leaving the room
like that." I would say that I was just going to
class, and she would say, "Girl, you could be
cute if you changed your style or did your
hair. You could get yourself a boyfriend!"
Finally, by Thanksgiving break, we came to
an understanding: She would never wear
Birkenstocks, and I would never wear tall, black,
leather boots. But as I left for break, she told me,
"Girl, do two things for yourself over break: Style
your hair, and buy black shoes."

—*SUMMER J.*
UNIVERSITY OF VIRGINIA, SENIOR

LAUNDRY 101

Just about the last thing I ever feel like doing in college is my laundry. Either I don't have quarters, don't have soap, or just don't care that my clothes are more wrinkled and dank than Bea Arthur on a humid day. If this sounds like you, try sticking to the following strategies for avoiding the laundry room:

For shirts, pants and the like, divide your clothes into two categories. Category One is the stuff you wear every day. Keep these items as clean as possible and when you're done wearing them, fold them neatly, put them in your drawer and pretend they're clean. A squirt of Fabreze might help as well.

Category Two is your "going out to parties clothes." This should be only one or two shirts and a pair of pants, which will stink of beer and smoke after a night out. Keep these in a trash bag on your closet floor. Wear them on Friday nights. No one will know the difference.

Tempting as it may be, you're not allowed to wear underwear twice. It's just wrong. You'll need to go to Wal-Mart and get 30 pairs of tightie-whities and 30 pairs of white tube socks. Wear each pair one day, and then once a month, throw all of them in the wash. It's all white, so you can do one load, and because it's just socks and underwear, you don't have to fold or sort anything. Just put them in another trash bag, next to your Friday night clothes. Keep two pairs of clean boxers on hand for dates.

—ADAM F.
GEORGE WASHINGTON UNIVERSITY, 2001

FRESHMEN ARE GENERALLY UPTIGHT about clothing; you always put on an "outfit" for class. After freshman year, you see people rolling into class with sweats or pajamas on (people really do wear pajama bottoms). In other countries it's an insult to dress like that, especially a sign of disrespect to a teacher or person in authority.

—*DIANA SHU*
UNIVERSITY OF CALIFORNIA AT BERKELEY, SOPHOMORE

. . . .

" Laundry is expensive, and you have to be careful because people will steal your stuff. I had a problem with that. I had to take my homework down there and do it while doing laundry. "

—*B.M.*
UNIVERSITY OF MARYLAND, JUNIOR

. . . .

ONE THING: I'M JAPANESE. It's important to buy clothes in the place where you are living, because it helps you fit in.

—*H.N.*
HARVARD UNIVERSITY, SENIOR

. . . .

USE MOM'S LAUNDRY DETERGENT and fabric softener to make your dorm room smell a little bit more like home!

—*LAURA WOLTER*
UNIVERSITY OF TEXAS AT AUSTIN, 1997

I'VE BEEN DOING MY OWN LAUNDRY since I was 12, but in college, I got a really big laundry bag and saved it and took it home, an hour and a half away.

—*MELISSA K. BYRNES*
AMHERST COLLEGE, 2000

• • • • • • • •

GET A LAUNDRY SERVICE. People will take your clothes out of the washer and dryer.

—*J.G.*
GEORGE WASHINGTON UNIVERSITY, SENIOR

• • • • • • • •

I HAD NEVER DONE LAUNDRY before in my life, but it's not that bad. Wash in cold water.

—*KATHY*
UNIVERSITY OF DELAWARE, FRESHMAN

• • • • • • • •

FOR LAUNDRY, I WAIT UNTIL I HAVE NO CLOTHES left, and then I do two big loads all at once and I'm done with it in a couple of hours.

—*ANONYMOUS*
UNIVERSITY OF PENNSYLVANIA, SOPHOMORE

• • • • • • • •

COLLEGE IS A GREAT PLACE TO MEET ALL KINDS of new people. But sometimes you can get into a rut—your daily routine becomes so regimented that you don't encounter as many new people as you did in the beginning. That's when its time to try something new or go someplace different. In my case, this was the laundry room. I found that on the rare occasions I went to the laundry room, I would make friends with one or two of the people waiting for their clothes to dry.

—*BRANDON WALKER*
JAMES MADISON UNIVERSITY, SOPHOMORE

Never wear anything from your high school. I mean, we all went to high school, but you don't have to advertise it.

—*J.T.*
UNIVERSITY OF FLORIDA, 1990

IN GENERAL I THINK IT'S PRETTY EASY, especially if you live in the dorm. Separate colors and whites. Just follow the instructions on the washing machine; do it one or two times and you'll be fine.

—*ALBERT LAI*
UNIVERSITY OF CALIFORNIA AT BERKELEY, SENIOR

• • • • • • • •

IF AT ALL POSSIBLE, GO TO A SCHOOL in a state where your grandmother lives an hour away and just take your laundry there. You need to visit her every once in a while, anyway. So take your laundry there; she'll cook you dinner.

—*ANONYMOUS*
UNIVERSITY OF VIRGINIA, SOPHOMORE

• • • • • • • •

FIND SOMEONE WHO REALLY KNOWS how to do laundry. You get here and you realize that you don't understand how not to dye all your clothes pink.

—*LUCY LINDSEY*
HARVARD UNIVERSITY, FRESHMAN

• • • • • • • •

✓ **CONTRARY TO THE LAUNDRY INDUSTRY'S CLAIMS,** all clothes can be washed and dried in one load. Over time, this will amount to a considerable saving, as well as create more time for partying.

—*BRIAN TURNER*
UNIVERSITY OF GEORGIA, 1996

• • • • • • • •

I FIND MYSELF BUYING UNDERWEAR instead of actually doing laundry. My advice is to wait until after the holidays and get the holiday packs of boxers for $1.99 at the Gap. I do that a lot. I have a lot of boxers with holly on them. And you can get a lot of free T-shirts from clubs.

—*MARTIN*
GEORGETOWN UNIVERSITY, SOPHOMORE

You meet people in the laundry room, so you can see it as a social experience.

—*H.P.*
UNIVERSITY OF PENNSYLVANIA FRESHMAN

FRESHMAN FACTOID

At the Graffiti Party at The Rose-Hulman Institute of Technology (Indiana), the dress code is simple: a plain white T-shirt, that is, so your artsy school-mates can deco-rate you with Magic Markers.

MY ROOMMATE NEVER CHANGED HER SHEETS. I loved her, but that was kind of gross. But, it was her bed. I say, change sheets at least every two weeks, probably every week. Wash everything in cold—nothing ever needs to be hot. I used to sep-arate, but now I don't. There's no need.

—*J.*
UNIVERSITY OF PENNSYLVANIA, JUNIOR

DON'T EVER LEAVE YOUR LAUNDRY; I got mine stolen. Someone had taken it out and people just went through my stuff and took what they wanted.

—*KRISTIN THOMAS*
JAMES MADISON UNIVERSITY, JUNIOR

• • • • • • • •

HANG UP CLOTHES IF THEY'RE NOT REALLY, really dirty. It keeps them from getting wrinkled.

—*JOEL*
PRINCETON UNIVERSITY, 2002

• • • • • • • •

MAKE FRIENDS WITH KIDS whose parents live close by and do laundry at their parents' house. I lugged laundry home on a two-hour train ride just so I didn't have to do it. It was a real pain. And do the essentials so that you don't run out of underwear and towels.

—*J.P.G.*
UNIVERSITY OF PENNSYLVANIA, SOPHOMORE

• • • • • • • •

BUY A LOT OF UNDERWEAR before you go. You can wear jeans until they walk. But you have to wash your underwear.

—*CHRISTINE*
UNIVERSITY OF RHODE ISLAND, SOPHOMORE

WHEN TO DO IT

Do laundry in the middle of the night or early in the morning—no one's there.

—*CASEY*
GEORGETOWN UNIVERSITY, SENIOR

• • • • • • • • •

Do not do laundry on Friday, Saturday, or Sunday. Wait until Monday, midday, when most people are at class. The maintenance staff has already fixed the machines from the weekend, and you don't have to worry about people taking your laundry out.

—*H.D. BALLARD*
UNIVERSITY OF VIRGINIA, FRESHMAN

• • • • • • • • •

Do your laundry in the middle of the week, not on the weekends.

—*KELLI*
UNIVERSITY OF DELAWARE, SOPHOMORE

• • • • • • • • •

I do laundry a lot, between classes in the morning or afternoon, during the week, and on the weekend. I do it whenever I can, to get it out of the way.

—*JENNIFER A. SICKLICK*
GEORGE WASHINGTON UNIVERSITY, FRESHMAN

• • • • • • • • •

I do my laundry Sunday morning. I set my alarm clock early. By the end of the week, all my clothes are dirty, and during the week I don't have time.

—*AMY HOFFBERG*
UNIVERSITY OF DELAWARE, FRESHMAN

• • • • • • • • •

Don't do laundry on Sunday. Everyone does it that day.

—*ANONYMOUS*
UNIVERSITY OF MARYLAND, SOPHOMORE

I **HEARD SOME HORROR STORIES** about people's roommates forgetting to wash their sheets. That will keep people out of your room.

—*MIKE PARKER*
  GEORGETOWN UNIVERSITY, SOPHOMORE

• • • • • • • •

YOU KNOW IT'S TIME TO DO LAUNDRY when you run out of underwear. I know guys who said it was time to do laundry when you've worn your underwear inside out. That's pretty gross.

—*NAT*
  UNIVERSITY OF RHODE ISLAND, SOPHOMORE

Free Time and How to Spend It

*L*et's see . . . go to class, eat, sleep . . . aren't you forgetting something? Oh, yeah; fun. Good times come in many flavors, as
you'll discover almost the minute you arrive on campus. Here's how
to stay well balanced, well honed, and ready for the next challenge.

FREE TIME: USE IT. Don't waste a drop. Don't sleep
your life away either! Enjoy any good weather
you get; study outdoors, play some wiffle ball,
anything to keep you busy. Or, use the time to get
ahead or catch up in classes. This will help your
G.P.A. immensely. Learn to balance your free time
between recreation and schoolwork and you can
be guaranteed a great college experience.

—*ARIEL MELENDEZ*
PRINCETON UNIVERSITY, FRESHMAN

**NEVER UNDER-
ESTIMATE THE
POWER OF A
TUESDAY NIGHT
GAME OF CARDS
IN THE DORM
ROOM.**

—*AMY FORBES*
*MISSISSIPPI STATE
UNIVERSITY, 2003*

MY FRESHMAN YEAR I TRIED ARCHERY and karate for the first time. I wasn't good at either of them, but it was fun being bad at something new.

We used to stay up at night when it was warm and sit on top of the parking garage. Some of the best times I had in college were up there, just talking. People talk more at night, especially when there are stars out.

—*AMY FORBES*
MISSISSIPPI STATE UNIVERSITY, 2003

· · · · · · · ·

I TRY NOT TO WASTE TIME. Work hard, play hard, is my attitude. Get your work done, then go out and have fun. There's definitely enough time in college to do what you need to do, as long as you're not watching TV.

—*JONATHAN GIFTOS*
BOSTON COLLEGE, SENIOR

· · · · · · · ·

Use the gym as much as possible, because when you get out, it's not free anymore. It's in your tuition so you're paying for it.

—*SANI G.*
UNIVERSITY OF
CALIFORNIA AT
IRVINE, JUNIOR

DON'T BE A WUSS YOUR FRESHMAN YEAR or you will have few friends. If you are the kind of kid who goes to bed at 10 o'clock, you will be in trouble. Learn to stretch yourself. Push yourself to be a late night party person or you will have no social life. Everyone walks around here deprived of sleep, but misery loves company. We have weekends to catch up.

—*TEJ SHAH*
CARNEGIE MELLON UNIVERSITY, SOPHOMORE

· · · · · · · ·

IT'S OK TO SAY NO. You don't have to do everything the first semester of your freshman year; you have seven more semesters to go. There's time. Pick one or two things that you're really passionate about. Then, go to your classes. Believe it or not, it's why we're here.

—*H.D. BALLARD*
UNIVERSITY OF VIRGINIA, FRESHMAN

CHECK THINGS OUT, PARTY-WISE, when you first get to college, because after a while it gets too crowded with work. You get too busy, so it's important to have fun at first.

> —*PATRICK*
> *UNIVERSITY OF RHODE ISLAND, FRESHMAN*

• • • • • • • •

SO MANY PEOPLE ARE SLEEP DEPRIVED that they become zombies. Once I woke up and went to class in the afternoon thinking it was morning; this is not unusual. People are always confused about dates and times. Learn how to survive without sleep and you will thrive in college.

> —*LINDSEY SHULTZ*
> *CARNEGIE MELLON UNIVERSITY, SENIOR*

• • • • • • • •

IT'S REALLY HARD TO PAY ATTENTION freshman year because of all the new influences. A lot of people are meeting every day and wanting to hang out every day. I couldn't balance all the work I had to do and still hang out with people, so I had to stop hanging out with so many people.

> —*R.S.*
> *HOWARD UNIVERSITY, SOPHOMORE*

• • • • • • • •

THE GREATEST THING WAS TAKING MUSIC; the camaraderie in general is great. I'm in a quartet and I'm in the orchestra. The orchestra was great in that you can play lots of different pieces that are new and keep up stuff that you've been doing for a while. In the quartet you get to know people on a very individual level and get to know how they play. You get to hang out with them at different times, so it just makes it that much more special. That was a big highlight of my year.

> —*IAN MOK*
> *HARVARD UNIVERSITY, SOPHOMORE*

It's very important to do something physical. That's how I release all my stress.

—*B.M.*
UNIVERSITY OF MARYLAND, JUNIOR

Don't let it all overwhelm you. For some kids, the freedom is intoxicating. A lot of kids are partying a lot.

You've got to crack down and be mature about it.

—*MATT MONACO
GEORGE
WASHINGTON
UNIVERSITY
FRESHMAN*

DO STUPID STUFF. One time our R.A. randomly said, "I'm going to the beach to go swimming, you want to go?" It was 2 a.m. in the fall and it was freezing cold. But we said, "OK." So we all went swimming in freezing water at 2 a.m. in the ocean—and I've never felt more alive. You'll never remember staying up and studying for a midterm. What you'll remember is staying up and doing something instead of studying.

—*MIKEY LEE
STANFORD UNIVERSITY, JUNIOR*

• • • • • • • •

SOMETIMES YOU NEED TIME to just sit down and do absolutely nothing and relax. That's the most valued time I have.

—*BRYAN
GEORGETOWN UNIVERSITY, SOPHOMORE*

• • • • • • • •

NOTHING IS BETTER THAN PLAYING FLAG FOOTBALL with a bunch of other washed-up, untalented, former high school football players. Another benefit to intramural sports: you can show up to the game drunk and nobody says anything!

Do things you never thought you would do. Ride the mechanical bull in that redneck bar, drink too much, and participate in karaoke. Do all these things while you can. Before you know it these behaviors will be frowned upon, so you need to get it out of your system.

—*P.G.
UNIVERSITY OF GEORGIA, 1999*

• • • • • • • •

KEEP YOUR HOBBIES—you'll have lots of free time that you'll otherwise waste.

—*D.D.
UNIVERSITY OF PENNSYLVANIA, 1989*

WAFFLE HOUSE WAS A GREAT WAY to wind down the evening before heading home for the night. My friends and I would always seem to end up there after a long night of going out at the bars. Upon arrival, we would always head straight for the jukebox. Once the quarters were in, the other Waffle House patrons were definitely in for a treat. We would sing mostly 1980s hits, ranging from "Jessie's Girl" to "867-5309." Depending on the crowd, we could sometimes get others to participate. It was definitely a sight to see.

—*JIMMY LYNCH*
  AUBURN UNIVERSITY, 2001

If you're an athlete, you have to learn to manage your time. Learn to rest, and learn when you can socialize.

—*JOHNATHAN J.*
  GEORGIA INSTITUTE OF TECHNOLOGY, JUNIOR

WHEN YOU HAVE FREE TIME, enjoy things that are non-school-related and healthy: Join a really random club, be in a play, volunteer, run a marathon, become a *film noir* enthusiast. Your free time can really give you a chance to meet people of similar mindset and interest, and can also expose you to interests and ideas you can't find in the lecture hall. Also, make sure you watch a little bit of TV now and then, to prevent college "bubble" syndrome.

—*AMY*
  PRINCETON UNIVERSITY, FRESHMAN

JOIN THE STUDENT UNION of your university or college. I found out too late that these are the cool folks who are planning and arranging what bands and movies come to the student center.

—*BRIAN TURNER*
UNIVERSITY OF GEORGIA, 1996

" "Try new things. I never acted in high school, but I tried out for a play and got one of the lead roles. It's a lot of fun. I'm going to do a lot more of that now. "

—*CONOR MCNEIL*
EMORY UNIVERSITY, SOPHOMORE

FIND A WAY TO RELAX AND GET AWAY; know when to let go. There are things that are hard to deal with and overwhelming. Know when to detach and say "whatever," and take it in stride.

—*MICHAEL GAY*
ST. LAWRENCE UNIVERSITY, SOPHOMORE

PLAY ULTIMATE FRISBEE; it's a good way to compete. You can't compete in most college sports unless you've played your entire life. If you want to play varsity soccer, you can't just do it. With Ultimate Frisbee, we take everybody. You don't have to be athletic or even have any experience in it. You learn everything and you play other colleges.

—*JOSH STAFFORD*
UNIVERSITY OF VIRGINIA, 2002

✓ **HAVE FUN DOING ANYTHING,** and just smile and laugh at least once a day. You've got to find ways to have fun and relax every day, or else you'll go nuts. You can tell the kids that don't: they just suck at life and are no fun to be around.

—*ANONYMOUS*
UNITED STATES MILITARY ACADEMY AT WEST POINT,
JUNIOR

• • • • • • • •

HOW COLLEGE STUDENTS SPEND FREE TIME

Activity	Women	Men
Go on the Internet	90%	80%
Talk on the phone	99%	99%
Watch TV	88%	82%
Listen to recorded music	86%	90%
Listen to the radio	86%	75%
Run errands	76%	70%
Hang out with friends	68%	63%
Exercise	52%	52%
Read a newspaper	40%	47%
Read a book	35%	32%
Watch videos/DVDs	34%	40%
Read magazines	34%	40%

• • • • • • • •

YOU'RE GOING TO BE AWAY from home for the first time in your life. Take it one step at a time; don't try to be completely independent. Experiment and do new things, but don't go overboard.

—*JERRY JUN*
EMORY UNIVERSITY, SENIOR

THERE'S SO MUCH AVAILABLE that you've always wanted to do, or that you've found interesting all of a sudden, but you can't try to do everything at once or else you're just going to get really overwhelmed and it's going to be really difficult to keep up with academics and extracurriculars at the same time. Focus on a specific thing that you want to do outside of your academics. That way you'll be able to do a few things at a high level, as opposed to many different things at a not-so-high level.

—*ALISON MILLER*
HARVARD UNIVERSITY, SOPHOMORE

• • • • • • • •

WALK TO CLASSES WHEN YOU CAN. It's good for you and it will give you a chance to get to know the campus. Notice the people around you. Take time out of your day to sit on a bench and look at your surroundings. Be friendly; make the effort to say hello, even if the other person looks grumpy.

—*J.S.*
UNIVERSITY OF GEORGIA, 1995

• • • • • • • •

IT'S REALLY HARD TO FIND TIME to be alone in college. You're always surrounded by people: your roommates, your friends, your classmates. In high school you have your own room; in college I always shared a room. It's important to find time to be alone so that you can reflect on everything you're going through. Go on walks, and write in a journal. If you go through your routine every day, the days pass so fast; if you don't think back on your day, it doesn't seem as meaningful. You don't treasure the memories that you make if you don't record them in a journal. In the future you'll be able to look back and see how your freshman year was. Try to find yourself and think about your experiences.

—*MEGHAN*
UNIVERSITY OF NOTRE DAME, JUNIOR

How do you survive freshman year? Nap. Get up for class. Go to class. Then nap. That's how you survive.

—*MIKEY LEE*
STANFORD UNIVERSITY JUNIOR

ON FREEDOM

I had a really smooth transition. My parents had given me a lot of independence at home, so I was used to not having very much supervision, and when I went to college it wasn't much different.

I know a lot of people who had really strict parents, and sometimes when your parents are too strict or too overbearing you don't learn how to deal with things yourself. So when you're left on your own and your parents aren't there—I mean, some parents still try to control you from really far away through the phone or whatever—you should really know what your values are and what you want to do. You need to know what your goals are, and be disciplined to do what you want and get what you want.

There are so many other distractions and there's nothing to really stop you—there are no parents—so have in mind what you're going to college for, and never lose sight of that.

First semester I was really there for the experience, because I had gotten straight A's in high school and I thought, "I'm not really going to worry about getting straight A's in college." So I took the first semester a lot more easily, and when I had the opportunity to go out and do something or have fun, I would do that rather than study. After I did that for a semester, I got more serious.

It's really about knowing when to draw the line. Every time you're faced with a decision you have to realize what it means.

—*ERIC CHENG*
HARVARD UNIVERSITY, SOPHOMORE

☆ **I RECOMMEND SELF-DEFENSE CLASSES** if they're offered. It makes you feel more aware and comfortable and confident. The more you're like that, the less likely it is that you'll be a target.

—*MELISSA K. BYRNES*
AMHERST COLLEGE, 2000

• • • • • • • • •

BEATS STUDYING

While you're cramming in the library, here's how some other freshmen around the country are spending their time:

Race track
   Washington State University
Toy design department
   Otis College (California)
Professional golf courses
   Purdue University (Indiana), Augusta State University (Georgia), Kent State University (Ohio)
Massage therapy room
   Baker College of Cadillac (Michigan)
International gaming institute
   University of Nevada-Las Vegas
Cross-country ski trails
   SUNY Oswego
Dance studio
   University of Tampa (Florida)
Rodeo arena
   Oklahoma Panhandle State University

• • • • • • • •

DOING A SPORT HELPS ME GET MY WORK DONE. It has given me more friends, and I got to start freshman year with a set group of friends.

—*SUSAN LIPPERT*
EMORY UNIVERSITY, JUNIOR

INTRODUCE YOURSELF TO EVERYONE; it makes a difference. If you continue to say hi to people, you'll get to know people. Not everyone will be your best friend, but you'll get there. You'll have new friends.

—*J. DEVEREUX*
GEORGETOWN UNIVERSITY, 2002

. . . .

"**People need to go out and party. Not necessarily go out and get drunk, but go out and have fun with friends. Do something you like to do. Don't do work all the time; there's more to life than that.**"

—*GREG*
JAMES MADISON UNIVERSITY, JUNIOR

. . . .

I WAS INVOLVED WITH THE CRISIS HOTLINE. The most common call that we had by far was what we called the loneliness call. It would be a person on a huge campus who felt lonely—a person who doesn't know how to meet people, who's away from home the first time.

My college has more than 250 student organizations—fraternities and sororities, hang-gliding club, bungee-jumping club, weight-lifting club, all kinds of ethnic organizations, every religious group. There has to be a group out there that has your interest.

—*MICHAEL A. FEKULA*
UNIVERSITY OF MARYLAND, 1985

THERE'S ALWAYS SOMEBODY AWAKE in the dorm that you can go talk to. We had 300 people in our dorm, so there was always somebody awake, doing something.

If you go out at night, your whole day the next day is killed. So we started doing different things. We started running races on Saturday mornings and things like that. It was more fun than going out and getting trashed.

—*S.L.R.*
UNIVERSITY OF VIRGINIA, SOPHOMORE

66 Take part in sports. It adds another element to college and makes you better adjusted. It also makes you more relaxed and more productive. 99

—*JOEL*
PRINCETON UNIVERSITY, 2002

STUDYING IN COLLEGE IS VERY HARD, so be careful taking care of your health. It's important to have time to refresh your mind. Find a social outlet. Do your work with friends; it makes it easier. Go to the gym, go hiking, meet other people. You talk about other topics and it takes your mind off your studies. You need that.

—*H.N.*
HARVARD UNIVERSITY, SENIOR

I FOUND MYSELF, FRESHMAN YEAR OF SCHOOL, suffering from Seasonal Affective Disorder due to my first experience in a location that featured long, cold winters. Having depression when you're at college (supposedly the best years of your life) sucks. Don't be afraid to check into the local tanning booth for some sun treatment. Don't be embarrassed about trying antidepressants. Or transfer to a college somewhere warm. I swear, my grades would have been better if I had gone to school somewhere less environmentally challenging.

> —*ANONYMOUS*

If your college has sports events, go to them. It's part of the college experience.

> —*ANONYMOUS*
> *UNIVERSITY OF*
> *MARYLAND*
> *SOPHOMORE*

• • • • • • • •

AT MY SCHOOL, one of the freshman traditions is to go in this fountain. By the end of my freshman year, I still hadn't gone in that fountain. One night, one of my guy friends and I decided to go. The fountain wasn't turned on, but we sat up at the top of this dry fountain for three or four hours. It was one of the best experiences. We talked about everything—our expectations for college and for life. I think we started to understand what life is really about.

> —*KERRY*
> *GEORGETOWN UNIVERSITY, 2002*

• • • • • • • •

FRESHMAN YEAR IS FUN. Everything is new and you make lots of new friends.
Sophomore year is less fun. There are no new people; you know everybody. You can get in a rut. So don't wait for other people and things to come to you; go out and do stuff. There's so much more at school than you can ever experience in four years. Go swimming.

> —*EDITH ZIMMERMAN*
> *WESLEYAN UNIVERSITY, SOPHOMORE*

IT'S TOUGH TO BALANCE doing a sport and being at school. You practice three hours a day, and you go to school all day. When you get home you're tired, and you have to find time to study. A lot of times you don't want to, but you have to learn how to do it. It took me all of first year to learn how. I mean, we're normal students in some ways, but in other ways we're not, because we're always doing something. We don't have the free time a lot of people do when they get out of class. When we get out of class, we have to go here and go there; we're traveling, we're on the road, we're in hotels. It's tough to make the grade when you play sports.

> —*RUSTY BENNETT*
> *GEORGIA STATE UNIVERSITY, SOPHOMORE*

SPORTS—I PLAYED A LITTLE BIT OF EVERYTHING in college. I had never played water polo in my life and I played that in intramurals and it was great. I played flag football, softball, volleyball; all that stuff. Sports are a great release. I played competitive sports in high school but I wasn't good enough to play on the college level, so it was a good way for a frustrated athlete to get out there and keep alive and be active. Intramurals were a way to be competitive, but it wasn't so competitive that you had to deal with the pressures.

> —*JOHN BENTLEY*
> *TRINITY UNIVERSITY, 1995*

DON'T BE AFRAID TO USE THE HEALTH CENTER, for both medical and mental problems. It's cheap, it's confidential, and it really can help if you get the blues.

> —*ANONYMOUS*
> *UNIVERSITY OF GEORGIA, 1995*

I GOT SICK MY FIRST YEAR. I didn't have anyone to supervise when I went to bed and what I ate. That's a learning-by-doing thing.

—*A.G.H.*
UNIVERSITY OF VIRGINIA, SENIOR

• • • • • • • •

ROOT FOR THE HOME TEAM (even if some of them have very strange names...)

Trolls—Trinity Christian College (Illinois)

Gorillas—Pittsburg State University (Kansas)

Rajin' Cajuns—University of Louisiana at Lafayette

Flames—Culinary Institute of America (New York)

Bombers—Ithaca College (New York)

Blue Hose—Presbyterian College (South Carolina)

Hardrockers—South Dakota School of Mines & Technology

Wasps—Emory & Henry College (Virginia)

Vixens—Sweet Briar College (Virginia)

Banana Slugs—University of California-Santa Cruz

Horned Frogs—Texas Christian University

• • • • • • • •

A DAILY NAP IS A GOOD IDEA. Come back from class and take a nap and you wake up and feel like it's a whole new day. An hour-long nap, or even a 15-minute power nap, is good.

—*WHITNEY*
YALE UNIVERSITY, FRESHMAN

COLLEGES WHERE SPORTS RULE

- University of Notre Dame (Indiana)

- Penn State

- University of North Carolina at Chapel Hill

- Duke University (North Carolina)

- Florida State University

• • • • • • • •

I JOINED CREW AND IT WAS FUN, but it was very time-consuming. I had to quit after my novice year; it hurt my grades. We had two practices every day and a meet on weekends. The practices were two hours, sometimes more. You had to get up at 5 a.m. and practice until 7:30 a.m., go to your 8 a.m. class, go through your day, then have another practice around 5 p.m. We had practice about every 12 hours. I recommend it, but be wary of the grade situation. If you can handle it, that's great. I wish I could've handled it; I loved it.

—DAVE
UNIVERSITY OF RHODE ISLAND, JUNIOR

On The Road Again: Trips, Vacations, and Studying Abroad

*Y*ou've *finally adjusted to college and here it is, time to break away. Whether it's a weekend, a holiday, or summer vacation, there are hazards as well as opportunities out there: Find out.*

IF IT'S NOT YOUR THING TO DRINK A LOT and do all that stuff, you probably won't enjoy spring break. You only get four spring breaks while you're in college. If you don't enjoy partying all the time, you're not going to enjoy it in Mexico after you spent $1,000.

—*JONATHAN COHEN*
EMORY UNIVERSITY, SENIOR

GO HOME FOR THE HOLIDAYS YOUR FRESHMAN YEAR.

—*SHANNON*
STANFORD UNIVERSITY SENIOR

SPRING BREAK IN MEXICO FRESHMAN YEAR was the best. There was this one guy who imitated a dancer at a club we went to, by putting on a thong and carrying a torch. He did this dance for 500 people at the pool and everyone loved it. He became a hero at our school and girls loved him. Go to spring break and distinguish yourself, and you will develop a reputation.

—*JAKE DENNE*
CARNEGIE MELLON UNIVERSITY, JUNIOR

" When you go to school overseas, you get a better perspective on the world. You don't see the world from an American point of view. It will help anybody. "

—*MICHAEL LANDIS GOGEL*
NEW YORK UNIVERSITY, SOPHOMORE

I WOULD RECOMMEND DRIVING your parents' van, with a nice bed in back, coast to coast, 3,000 miles. It doesn't take too long. I did that with my girlfriend. I learned to surf once I got to California. My parents didn't know I had taken the van until I was in another state. But when I called them, they said, "We've been waiting for you to do something like that." It was great.

—*STEVE BAKER*
COLUMBIA UNIVERSITY, SENIOR

MY JUNIOR YEAR, I TOOK ADVANTAGE of the "terms abroad" program and lived in Ecuador for a year. It was a phenomenal opportunity to study abroad. Life had seemed sort of small before that experience.

—*CALE GARAMANDI*
UNIVERSITY OF CALIFORNIA AT BERKELEY, JUNIOR

• • • • • • • •

BEST WEEKEND GETAWAY—CAMPING. It's cheap, it's fun, and all your friends will want to join you. Get a map of state campgrounds; a great weekend of hiking, nature, romance and s'mores may be just an hour's drive away.

—*WENDY W.*
UNIVERSITY OF GEORGIA, 1996

• • • • • • • •

I WENT HOME FOR THE HOLIDAYS MY FRESHMAN YEAR, and I think it was a good thing, because it can just get really crazy. Everything is so new and so exciting and there are so many people that you feel like you're at camp for an extended period of time. It depends on what your home situation is like, but it's important to keep in touch with your parents; it helps remind you that you're actually here to do something. For me, keeping in touch with my parents kept a balanced view; you should explore, but keep your feet on the ground, too.

—*SHANNON*
STANFORD UNIVERSITY, SENIOR

• • • • • • • •

STUDYING ABROAD WAS A FANTASTIC EXPERIENCE, learning the culture of the British people, learning so much about a different way of studying, a different school system, and a different language in England. It's a valuable opportunity and experience.

—*C.W.*
RHODES COLLEGE, SENIOR

Advice to the guys: Go on a cruise for spring break. The odds are unbelievable! You will be amazed at the ratio.

—*JIMMY LYNCH*
AUBURN UNIVERSITY
2001

SETTING AN EXAMPLE

One of the most memorable times I had in college was a road trip to New York City with about five pals, an idea hatched at 10 p.m., executed immediately, and celebrated in Central Park in the wee hours. We all flopped on the floor at a friend's place at Columbia University, partied some more with him, and woke up in a stupor. The highlight was a morning visit to the home of one of the pals, the only son of a working-class couple in Queens. In that cramped apartment, during the time it took to eat a carefully pre-pared breakfast, we observed in utter awe the incredible, unfettered love of a mother and father for their

son. They were so proud of their boy. It wasn't so much in what they said, but the ambience, the pictures on the mantle, the beam in dad's eye, the doting by the mother. There was nothing overpowering or unbalanced or pushy about it; it was a natural pride and confidence in their son. For me, there have been few times when I was inspired by the human condition; this was one of them.

—R.S.
GEORGETOWN UNIVERSITY, 1990

TAKE A FUN JOB IN THE SUMMER after your freshman year; you deserve the break. I couldn't stand the thought of being at home all summer, living with a curfew, so a friend and I went to Orlando for the summer and got a job at Disney World. We didn't make any money, after paying our apartment and expenses, but we met lots of people and had a good time.

—*K.E.R.*
FLORIDA STATE UNIVERSITY, 1997

• • • • • • • •

THE LESS OFTEN YOU GO HOME your freshman year, the better. The more you're at school your freshman year, the more you're going to make friends and have people to hang out with after that. Your ties from home are going to break anyway. The sooner you do it, the better off you are.

—*BETHANY*
JAMES MADISON UNIVERSITY, SENIOR

• • • • • • • •

GO TO ITALY. Spend a semester there. I did, and it completely changed my outlook on life. Before I went, I was only interested in the American college existence: partying, getting by, attending football games. After I got back, I wanted to learn more, to be more.

—*M.A.*
FLORIDA STATE UNIVERSITY, 1991

• • • • • • • •

GOING HOME AFTER FRESHMAN YEAR was a big adjustment; not being surrounded by all my friends, being the only one awake after 10 p.m. I don't think I had much fun that summer, which is why the last few summers I've stayed at school. But I think all the vacations and other chances you have to go home are a good time to reflect on your freshman year.

—*T.P.*
STANFORD UNIVERSITY, SENIOR

Bring friends home for the holidays. Your family and your friends will remember it forever.

—*D.D.*
UNIVERSITY OF PENNSYLVANIA 1989

⭐ **IF SOMEONE YOU KNOW OFFERS** to have you to stay with her over a break, take her up on it. One of the most interesting experiences I had was staying with the parents of a roommate or friend, and discovering what her life was like before I met her. It is really mind-expanding, and allows you to get to know someone in your life even better. You also have the added bonus of a personal tour guide to show you around. Nothing is more fun than rediscovering where you have lived for your whole life by showing your college friends all of the tourist destinations.

—*AMY*
PRINCETON UNIVERSITY, FRESHMAN

• • • • • • • •

DOESN'T FEEL LIKE SCHOOL

Where can you get that vacation feeling without having to leave campus?

• **Beach house**—The Citadel (South Carolina)

• **Wilderness cabin**—Linfield College (Oregon)

• **Research boat**—Hawaii Pacific University

• **2 private beaches and a private dock with a fleet of sail-boats**—Mitchell College (Connecticut)

• **20-foot boat "for marine studies"**—Muhlenberg College (Pennsylvania)

• **29,000-acre experimental forest**—University of Montana

• • • • • • • •

I WENT TO NIGER FOR A SEMESTER. It was amazing. The academics are not a priority, but the cultural experience shifted my direction, what I want to get involved in.

—*MAYA MOORE*
GEORGETOWN UNIVERSITY, SENIOR

I WENT ON A SEMESTER-LONG TRIP on a cruise ship. It's a program where professors from around the country come and teach everything from anthropology to music to economics. We went to ten countries around the world. It's the most amazing opportunity ever. You get to learn about countries from a very non-Western point of view. I went to a wild game reserve in South Africa and visited the sand people that live on the outskirts. We learned about them and they sold us their wares. We went skydiving. We went to Carnival in Rio. When you're a freshman you should plan to do something like that; it had such an impact on me.

—MAYTAL AHARONY
GEORGE WASHINGTON UNIVERSITY, SENIOR

" Don't go home on the weekends. Stay at college as much as you can as a freshman, to get to know people and get a feeling for what's going on. I went home for the first part of the semester my freshman year, and then I started staying. I enjoyed college a lot more when I stayed. "

—MATT BIGGERSTAFF
EMORY UNIVERSITY, SENIOR

DO TAKE THOSE LAST-MINUTE ROAD TRIPS; they're the most fun. My freshman year, on a whim, a group of friends and I decided to go to the New Order concert at a college campus hundreds of miles away. We caravanned down, stayed with some friends, and went to the concert the next night. It was so much fun.

—K.E.R.
FLORIDA STATE UNIVERSITY, 1997

• • • • • • • •

When you see the world from a different perspective, you realize what you can be.

—M.A.
FLORIDA STATE UNIVERSITY, 1991

I GOT INVOLVED IN SERVICE WORK, traveling to other countries. I've been to Mexico and down south to North Carolina for Habitat for Humanity. That's defined my college career, my transformation. It gave me a better appreciation for my position in the world and at the same time for others in the world who don't have as much as I do. It's been an enlightening experience. But I've still had plenty of time to party.

—JONATHAN GIFTOS
BOSTON COLLEGE, SENIOR

Friends: Good, Better, Best, or Former

*L*eaving your high school gang is one of the hardest things about your new college experience. But college friends often turn out to be friends for life, and many of those friendships are born in your freshman year.

CHECK YOUR EMAIL EVERY DAY. And IM is a must; I message all my friends. It's one of the first things you do when you meet someone. You exchange room numbers and phone numbers, and then after you start talking, you ask for their screen name so you can tell each other about parties or when you're going to dinner. It's on all the time. I leave an away message: I'm at class, I'll be back at 2 p.m. That way, people don't call you worrying where you are.

—*AMY HOFFBERG*
UNIVERSITY OF DELAWARE, FRESHMAN

IT TAKES TIME TO MEET GOOD FRIENDS.
—*ZAK AMCHISLAVSKY*
GEORGETOWN UNIVERSITY, SENIOR

DON'T BURN BRIDGES WITH PEOPLE. You might not like them, but give it a year or two before you discard them.

—JOSH HERN
PURDUE UNIVERSITY, 1998

• • • • • • • •

MEET AS MANY PEOPLE AS YOU CAN. Be friendly and outgoing and people will be attracted to you; you'll have a much better time overall. Balance is the key to maintaining grades, relationships, and sanity. Be sure to get yourself plenty of that balance thing . . .

—ARIEL MELENDEZ
PRINCETON UNIVERSITY, FRESHMAN

• • • • • • • •

WHILE MY HIGH SCHOOL FRIENDS are not as involved in what I am trying to do as my Curtis friends, they remain my truest of friends. They represent a place where I can come anytime and be comfortable. They pick me up from school, they sit through concerts full of music they don't really like—they are my true friends.

—N.
CURTIS INSTITUTE OF MUSIC, SOPHOMORE

• • • • • • • •

IT'S BETTER TO ROOM WITH A HIGH SCHOOL FRIEND and get to know the guys around the hall sooner, without having to get to know your roommate. High school friends are great for meeting new people; most of my friends were guys I met through a high school friend in another dorm. Of course, there's always the junior or senior you know from high school, who usually is 21 and has a nice apartment or house; if they don't mind, that's a good place to hang out on the weekends.

—DAN
MIAMI UNIVERSITY, FRESHMAN

Stay open. You are going to meet so many different people every day. Just stay open.

—LINA J.
GEORGIA STATE UNIVERSITY
SOPHOMORE

IT'S VERY EASY FOR A GIRL to find guy friends. My freshman year all my friends at first were guys. I loved the attention and they were cool to hang out with. But while other girls were making friendships with girls that were solid, I was not. So when I hit a rough time and needed a female shoulder to cry on, it was not there. This was a big mistake I paid for dearly.

—*KAROLINE EVANS*
CARNEGIE MELLON UNIVERSITY, JUNIOR

• • • • • • • •

LOOK FOR SOMEONE WHO is on the same schedule as you: sleep, waking up, work.

—*ANONYMOUS*
UNITED STATES MILITARY ACADEMY AT WEST POINT
JUNIOR

• • • • • • • •

Surround yourself with good people. It's more about quality than quantity when it comes to friends.

—*JESSICA*
BARNARD COLLEGE
JUNIOR

GOING HOME FOR THE FIRST TIME is a combination of the best and worst feelings you will ever have. Although it is fabulous to hook back up with the old crowd, party where you used to, and possibly rediscover that old flame, it is also very hard to realize that every one of your friends now has a life that is completely separate from your experience. Sometimes reuniting is not the celebration you thought it would be. Acknowledge your differences, and enjoy your friends for who they are. Look at photos, hear crazy stories, and go out and have fun together, but always remember that things have changed (which is not necessarily a bad thing). And never go back to the old ex; it only ends in trouble.

—*A.*
PRINCETON UNIVERSITY, FRESHMAN

I HANG OUT WITH ABOUT FIVE PERCENT of the people that I hung out with freshman year. You hung out with them because you had to spend time with them, they were on your floor. But then you figure out who you like.

—*ZAK AMCHISLAVSKY*
GEORGETOWN UNIVERSITY, SENIOR

• • • • • • • •

66 Don't spend too much time with your high school friends. Half my high school ended up going to my college. I was fortunate enough to live on the other side of campus. They're still hanging out with each other. They've never met other people and they all live together. 99

—*R.S.*
UNIVERSITY OF MARYLAND, JUNIOR

Try to be more outgoing than you normally are. Be open to more things than you normally would.

—*M.D.*
BOSTON COLLEGE
FRESHMAN

• • • • • • • •

DEFINITELY KEEP IN TOUCH with your high school friends. You can always count on them for support and good laughs. This may be stating the obvious, but when you return home, they'll be the first ones (aside from your family) who will want to spend time with you and with whom you will most likely socialize, so why fall out of touch?

—*ARIEL MELENDEZ*
PRINCETON UNIVERSITY, FRESHMAN

✔ **WHEN I MET MY BEST FRIEND,** she was crying in her bed in our freshman dorm. She had a long-distance boyfriend. She was from the mountains of Georgia. I'm from St. Louis. I went to a private, Catholic girl's school. She went to a public school with rednecks and people with gun racks on their cars. We couldn't be more different. But we had a class together and one day, after I found her crying, she overslept. So I was like, "Oh, I'll call you in the morning," and we started walking to class together, and we got breakfast after class. We became friends.

—J. DEVEREUX
GEORGETOWN UNIVERSITY, 2002

• • • • • • • •

INVITE YOUR HIGH SCHOOL FRIENDS over for a couple of days. The ones who stay in touch are the ones worth keeping for a lifetime.

—KHALIL SULLIVAN
PRINCETON UNIVERSITY, JUNIOR

• • • • • • • •

IM IS THE ONLY WAY I STAY IN CONTACT with some people. It's an amazing invention; I use it all the time. But it can suck you in. Yesterday, I stayed off it for the first time in a week; I guess I realized I needed to do some college stuff. But it helps you adjust to college life. Back home, I have a lot of friends I want to stay in touch with. I have one life back home and now I'm starting up a new life. In the beginning it's hard; you want to maintain your old life. But you also have to realize that you're maturing and changing. IM is kind of a bridge between these two worlds.

—MATT MONACO
GEORGE WASHINGTON UNIVERSITY, FRESHMAN

WHAT KIND OF FISH ARE YOU?

Little pond? California's Deep Springs College has 26 undergraduates

Big pond? The University of Texas at Austin has 37,155 undergraduates.

Make sure you have some good friends around.

—*Laura Gzyzewski*
DeSales University
Junior

I didn't click with the other freshmen all that much. It was a different culture. The kids at my college are a lot better off than I was; they have a lot more money, so they go out and party all the time. That's something I never really did. I didn't feel like going out shopping at J.Crew and Abercrombie & Fitch all that much. I had to find people that did things that were comfortable for me.

—*Johnny*
Georgetown University, Junior

• • • • • • • •

Make real efforts to be with your friends, even if you're just doing dumb stuff like watching a movie or painting your nails. This is the only time in life where you'll be living with all your friends, and you'll miss it when it's gone. One of my best friends and I make a date every week to do our nails and talk; it's something you need to do anyhow, and it's so much more fun if you get to spend quality time and gossip with one of your favorite people. College can get really hectic: it's nice to know that some things can stay constant.

—*Julie*
Princeton University, Sophomore

Family Ties

Y*ou've spent almost 18 years trying to convince your family to let you do your own thing. . .and now you're on your own and maybe you miss them. It's strange how life works. How does your family fit into your new world? Years of experience (and lots of moms and dads, brothers and sisters) are shared below, and can help you keep the best and leave the rest behind.*

MAKE IT CLEAR TO PARENTS and grandparents that surprise visits are not a good idea, given how often you will be at the library.

—D.D.
UNIVERSITY OF PENNSYLVANIA, 1989

WHEN YOUR PARENTS VISIT, JUST LET THEM BABY YOU.

—M.A.
FLORIDA STATE UNIVERSITY, 1991

I BECAME A LOT CLOSER WITH MY PARENTS after going to college; I think a lot of students do. When you leave home, you hit a point of self-sufficiency. Parents start to respect your opinions more—once they come to grips with the fact that you're growing up, and once you've come to grips with the fact that you're growing up. I saw this chart once that showed that parents know everything when you're a little kid, then they start to not know as much. And by the time you get to high school, you hate them. But when you get into college, that chart starts to go back again to the beginning. I agree with that. The older you get, the more you understand where they were coming from.

—*Zach Friend*
University of California at Santa Cruz, 2001

• • • • • • • •

❝Do a lot of things your mother would disapprove of. Tattoos, body piercing, spring break trips; as long as you can act like an adult, the sky's the limit.❞

—*Anonymous*
Mississippi State University

• • • • • • • •

Ask for care packages. I loved receiving cookies and photos every now and then, and this lets your parents remain part of your life even if you are far away.

—*Amy*
Princeton University, Freshman

CALL YOUR PARENTS EVERY SINGLE WEEK, but you don't have to tell them everything. I call my mother on Sundays and talk to her for an hour and I'll catch her up with the things she will not be judgmental about. And the other stuff, I just don't tell her anymore. Pick and choose what you tell your parents.

—*CATE*
BROWN UNIVERSITY, JUNIOR

• • • • • • • •

I HATE TO ADMIT IT, BUT FRESHMAN YEAR I learned that when my parents tell me something, they may actually be right, and I realized that I should start to listen to what they say, especially since they have much more life experience than I do.

—*STEPHANIE KLEINER*
UNIVERSITY OF DELAWARE, SENIOR

• • • • • • • •

SET UP ONE NIGHT A WEEK WHEN YOU CALL YOUR PARENTS. Then they're not calling you every day and you're not calling them every day; that's not healthy for anyone.

—*J.G.*
GEORGE WASHINGTON UNIVERSITY, SENIOR

• • • • • • • •

I'M FROM L.A. and I have no family up here, so the transition from having a lot of family to not having anybody was tough. My mom used to call me twice a day—once at noon and once around 9 or 10 at night, just to check in on me, and say, "Where are you?" And I'd say, "I'm out." She'd be okay as long as I wasn't doing anything bad. I think about it and I think it was a good thing that she gave me a call every day, even though sometimes it was an invasion.

—*EDUARDO CHOZA*
SAN FRANCISCO STATE, SOPHOMORE

My parents get their two calls a week and that's about all they're going to get right now. It's the best way to do it.

—*WALTER*
UNIVERSITY OF MARYLAND COLLEGE PARK SOPHOMORE

MY MOM CALLS ME THREE TIMES A DAY. It's good to use the excuse that you're studying if you don't feel like talking. When I was a freshman, my roommate and I had this deal where we'd say, "Oh, my roommate didn't tell me you called." You invent little lies to keep them at bay.

—*J.*
BARNARD COLLEGE, JUNIOR

• • • • • • • •

I'M CLOSE TO MY PARENTS. We talk on the phone every other night and my mom IM's me. I don't think you should keep your parents at bay; my parents really helped me. They're very support-ive, and when you don't have anyone else there for you, they help you through your hard times. In college it's important to have your parents in your life, because we may think that we're really mature and know everything, but a lot of times they give you really good advice. They've been there before. In college, your parents are finally honest with you. In high school, they're like, "I never drank." Then in college, they're like, "This one time, I did this. You never want to do that." They become more human and less authoritarian. They help you.

—*ALYSSA*
JAMES MADISON UNIVERSITY, SOPHOMORE

• • • • • • • •

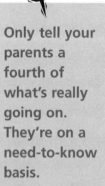

Only tell your parents a fourth of what's really going on. They're on a need-to-know basis.

—*J.G.*
FLORIDA STATE UNIVERSITY, 1991

I'M HISPANIC and I have really close ties with my family. I get along well with my parents and my little brother is my best friend. It was hard to say goodbye. I talk with them a lot. I call them on my cell phone like every other day, and talk for 45 minutes to an hour. And I email my little brother.

—*CESAR*
YALE UNIVERSITY, FRESHMAN

MY DAD IS KIND OF OLD-FASHIONED. Before I went to school he didn't even want me to have an ATM card. Then in the dorms, everyone had a mini-fridge. My dad said no to that, too. But I eventually won on both counts. College has changed so much that you should be patient with your parents, as they don't always understand the needs of today's freshmen. It might even be a good idea to give them a list of must-haves for freshmen: Cell phones, computers, Internet, beepers, etc.

—*A. ROSEN*
UNIVERSITY OF FLORIDA, 1995

• • • • • • •

"I never got homesick, but staying close to my parents and siblings definitely kept me sane over the course of freshman year."

—*PETE*
PRINCETON UNIVERSITY, SOPHOMORE

• • • • • • • •

ONCE I GOT TO COLLEGE, I curtailed all contact with home. I didn't call home as often as we agreed; sometimes I just wouldn't call home at all. My parents really worried. In retrospect I really regret that, because I put them through a lot of shit doing that. That's definitely a resolution for next year—to be more up on it when it comes to communication with back home.

—*F.S.*
STANFORD UNIVERSITY, SOPHOMORE

IT'S GOOD TO SHARE YOUR EXPERIENCES with your parents, but not all your experiences. Part of becoming your own person is having your own secrets and your own personal business. But if you share with your parents the things that fascinate you about growing up and being an adult, then that strengthens your bond. And they remember that they were kids once too; they remember how it was.

—*SHELBY NOEL HARRINGTON*
UNIVERSITY OF CALIFORNIA AT SANTA BARBARA, FRESHMAN

● ● ● ● ● ● ● ●

"Whenever you think about old friends or family, call them or write them right then. If you put it off you'll get preoccupied with a million other things and never get to it. So every time you think of someone, let them know—make it a first priority and do it—even if it's been a long time. "

—*AUBREY WALKER*
SANTA BARBARA CITY COLLEGE, SOPHOMORE

GRANDMA KNOWS BEST

It was the second half of my freshman year and I had my first hangover. My friends and I were at a concert and we were all drinking. I couldn't tell exactly what I drank and how much, but I tried anything and everything. It's all about discovering what you like and what you don't like, right? The next morning when I woke up, before I even opened my eyes, my head was throbbing. I hadn't eaten anything and my stomach and I were definitely not on speaking terms. I called my grandmother and asked her if she had ever experienced a hangover. She said, "Yes." I then told her I was having one. She laughed and came over to my apartment to comfort me. It's funny; I was 18 and thought I knew it all, but once I got my first hangover, who did I go running to? My grandmother! Keep close ties with your family as you may need them at any time.

—STEPHANIE M. MCKNIGHT
FROSTBURG STATE UNIVERSITY, SENIOR

Go to school away from home and away from your parents. But let them into your life. Be friends with them.

—*GINGER M. BRODTMAN SPRING HILL COLLEGE, 1998*

I TALK TO MY PARENTS A LOT AT NIGHT. Last night was the season premiere of *The West Wing*. I used to watch that with my dad a lot, so I called him before and after. And besides that, I talk to them twice a week just to catch up and see how it's going. It was my little brother's birthday and I wished him a happy birthday.

—*MATT MONACO GEORGE WASHINGTON UNIVERSITY, FRESHMAN*

• • • • • • • •

I'M REALLY CLOSE TO MY FAMILY. They drove me up here and we all cried. After they left, I was excited to be at school. I was ready to get away from my parents, experience life by myself, and be able to make my own decisions. I immediately had 25 friends, which were the girls on my hall, so I didn't miss them at first. But by mid-semester I was extremely homesick. I suddenly realized that my life was never going to be the same. I called home a lot and talked to my parents all the time. My dad emailed me every single day, and he always said, "P.S. Take your vitamins, go to church, and pray." Talking to them really helped me.

—*A.G.H. UNIVERSITY OF VIRGINIA, SENIOR*

• • • • • • • •

IF YOU GO HOME FOR THE SUMMER, make sure you go on vacation. I had to take trips by myself because I cannot be around my parents all the time. I realize they are real people and not all their habits are ones I want to live with. Separating from your parents is part of growing up and becoming a better person. You have to figure out what you want to be as a person, as opposed to what your parents are.

—*S. UNIVERSITY OF CALIFORNIA AT SANTA BARBARA, FRESHMAN*

✓ **YOU'VE GOT TO BE HONEST WITH YOUR PARENTS.** You've got to break them in. If you do bad stuff, you got to let them know; they're going to find out anyway, so you might as well be honest about it. If you tell them the way it is, they'll get used to it.

When you're visiting your parents you have to go by their rules in their house, but at the same time you can't be expected to follow every rule, especially if you're a college student.

—*BETH*
DIABLO VALLEY COLLEGE, FRESHMAN

• • • • • • • •

66 The thing with parents is that, nine times out of ten, they love you and they want to help you. If they get a little protective when you go away, it's because they don't know how to deal with it. Help them through it. Be patient with them. 99

—*B.*
GEORGE WASHINGTON UNIVERSITY, SENIOR

• • • • • • • •

YOUR PARENTS WILL LET GO of a lot once you leave for college, but swearing (especially f-bombs) when you're home on visits won't be well received.

—*D.D.*
UNIVERSITY OF PENNSYLVANIA, 1989

I HAVE CALLER ID ON MY CELL PHONE. If my parents call, I can see it's them and let it ring. But they email every day, too. They don't do IM because I haven't taught them that yet and they haven't figured it out. They say, "When you talk to people online, what does that mean?" And I say, "Oh, I just email them."

—*W.*
YALE UNIVERSITY, FRESHMAN

• • • • • • • •

MY RELATIONSHIP WITH MY PARENTS has improved a lot over the phone versus in person.

—*CHANA WEINER*
BARNARD COLLEGE, SOPHOMORE

Going Out, Hooking Up: Dating and Sex

*A*t first, college may seem like a supermarket of opportunities for dating and romance. But can you date the girl down the hall? Can upperclassmen be trusted? Should you stay true to your high-school sweetheart? Read a chapter from this book of experience.

DON'T BELIEVE THAT AN UPPERCLASSMAN is going to call you for a date, like he says he's going to. Don't wait by the phone. He gets drunk at frat parties and hooks up with the first thing he sees; that's how guys "date" in college.

—*K.E.R.*
FLORIDA STATE UNIVERSITY, 1997

YOU NEED TO GO OUT AND PARTY AND MEET LOTS OF PEOPLE.

—*ANONYMOUS*
YALE UNIVERSITY
SOPHOMORE

I HAD A BOYFRIEND FROM HOME, which was a big mistake. It kept me tied to home a little too much. I went a full year before we broke up. And I didn't party that much because of the boyfriend. I didn't drink at all in high school and that took a year to kick in, too. Then I was just like, screw it, I'm going to go out and have fun.

—*LYNN SNIFFEN*
BOSTON COLLEGE, JUNIOR

• • • • • • • •

66 Our dorm was arranged in suites; there were 18 people sharing a living room and a restroom. It was pretty much understood that you don't have a relationship with a suite mate because that was bad. That would cause horrible conflicts for everybody else in the group. 99

—*D.H.*
UNIVERSITY OF CALIFORNIA AT BERKELEY, 2000

• • • • • • • •

BE CAREFUL WHAT BRIDGES YOU CHOOSE to burn; you never know who's spreading rumors to whom.

—*ADAM*
ELON UNIVERSITY, SOPHOMORE

A GREAT PLACE TO MEET GIRLS is at the bookstore. Upon receiving the class syllabus, you have to buy books. If you're in the bookstore and you see a girl buying books, it's an easy entrance: "Oh, are you taking History of whatever . . ." Also, because I was at an all-guys school (Columbia), I'd go over to Barnard's cafeteria for lunch. When you're standing behind a girl in a cafeteria line, it's relatively easy to strike up conversation: "I see you like green Jello..."

—*J.R.*
COLUMBIA UNIVERSITY, 1986

• • • • • • • •

YOUR FIRST SEMESTER, DON'T DATE. You're still trying to get settled in college, you're making some new friends, you're dealing with all the anxiety of being away from your family and high-school friends, you're trying to get into classes that are much harder than you've had before. There's a lot of stress that first semester. Whether you're a guy or girl, you've got four or five years, and maybe after college, to meet the right person. Enjoy the freedom and you'll have a lot more fun that way.

—*C.W.*
RHODES COLLEGE, SENIOR

• • • • • • • •

DON'T EVER LISTEN TO what any college guy says. They all lie—about everything. Especially if they say, "Let's go for a walk." That's the worst: Run screaming.

Every girl needs to know how to punch so she can stick up for herself. Girls have to be tough: physically tough to kick someone's butt if you have to, and mentally tough to be able to say no.

—*JENNIFER SPICER*
FOOTHILL COLLEGE, 2000

Roller-skating, bowling, and getting ice cream cones are still great dates in college. In fact, you get major points for being bold enough to do them with gusto.

—*BRIAN TURNER*
UNIVERSITY OF GEORGIA, 1996

ADVICE FOR THE DATELORN

It's a mistake to start dating the first few weeks of college. I mean, compared to high school, college is paradise for dating: you're surrounded by people with your interests, you can stay up late, go to parties whenever you want, you can sleep together and not worry about parents—it's amazing. But be patient. There's this huge rush to date someone, but it's important to make friends first. That way, when you break up with someone, you still have your friends. If you start dating someone right away, you may miss out on making real friends, and that's more important.

Date someone who is also a freshman. In the first few months of school, it's hard to really relate to someone who's older. Plus, if you date someone who's older, it takes you away from your dorm and first-year activities; it almost makes you skip your first year. If you date someone who is also a freshman, you can go through freshman year together.

—SUMMER J.
UNIVERSITY OF VIRGINIA, SENIOR

DON'T MAKE DATING SO IMPORTANT. But if someone rocks your world, let nature take its course. I know a lot of girls who sweat guys and say how they want to get with the seniors. But it's not necessary.

—*KAROLYN*
UNIVERSITY OF MARYLAND, BALTIMORE COUNTY, SENIOR

· · · · · · · ·

❝If someone gets you alone, and gets the room all comfy and dim, and asks if you like Beefeater, please run screaming for eight miles in the opposite direction. They don't just mean gin, no matter what they say.❞

—*KARLA SAIA*
SAN DIEGO STATE UNIVERSITY, JUNIOR

· · · · · · · ·

DON'T COME WITH A GIRL FRIEND from home. There are several reasons. First, this is the first time you will really taste freedom and you do not want to be limited and restrained by someone from home. Second, there is booze and parties everywhere. You will feel like you are in a candy store. And you will see girls who are not the girl you grew up with. Everyone is insecure and looking for a connection.

—*DEREK LI*
CARNEGIE MELLON UNIVERSITY, JUNIOR

At a party, you usually ask a girl for her cell phone number, but asking her if she has a screen name isn't bad, either.

—PATRICK
   UNIVERSITY OF
   RHODE ISLAND
   FRESHMAN

HAVE A STRONG GROUP OF GIRLFRIENDS, then go meet guys and date. It can be a little confusing; you'll have to deal with a broken heart. That's where the girlfriends come in; they'll talk you through and just be there for you.

—*H.P.*
   UNIVERSITY OF PENNSYLVANIA, FRESHMAN

• • • • • • • •

IF YOU HAVE A BOYFRIEND AT HOME, get rid of him: You're going to stay in your dorm, you're not going to do anything, you're not going to meet new people; you're not going to live your life.

—*AMBER WITTEN*
   LOS MEDANOS COLLEGE, SOPHOMORE

• • • • • • • •

DON'T SET A HIGH EXPECTATION on getting laid.

—*M.*
   DUKE UNIVERSITY, 1984

• • • • • • • •

SOME GUYS ARE GREAT; some guys are not so great. Coming to school, no one has a past; people are going to be pushing the image they want you to see. So many people put up a front. They are who they're not. You can't possibly trust someone if you've just met them, so take time to get to know people. And don't have a relationship your first semester.

—*KERRY*
   GEORGETOWN UNIVERSITY, 2002

YOU WANT TO KNOW HOW TO GET GIRLS? Respect them. Be nice to them; it's that simple. Forget pickup lines or getting them drunk. In fact, warn them about guys like that. It sounds silly, but be their hero by being nice and thinking of them. Also, never, ever, ever try a pickup line, unless you're just kidding around. They never work. The only pickup line that works is, "Hi. How are you?" It's a legitimate start to a conversation.

—*R.B.*
MASSACHUSETTS INSTITUTE OF TECHNOLOGY, JUNIOR

· · · · · · · ·

❝The biggest thing I told myself was to put the whole boyfriend thing on hold. I figured it would be too much of a distraction to have a significant other. That helped.❞

—*JERI D. HILT*
HOWARD UNIVERSITY, SENIOR

· · · · · · · ·

GIRLS, YOU'VE GOT A ZONE. The first month, you're automatically going to fall in love with someone. Just keep your eyes open and don't get locked into anything.

My perception of college came from everything I saw on TV. I thought, it's going to be easy to get girls. It turns out it is easy, but you've still got to work. I thought being at college, girls would just flock to you, but it's not really the case.

—*KENTON*
UNIVERSITY OF VIRGINIA, SENIOR

More Wisdom

Be careful about dating too many older men when you're 18. Make sure they're actually going to your school.

—ANONYMOUS
CALVIN COLLEGE
2000

BE PREPARED TO MEET NO WOMEN your freshman year who want to date you. They are just not available. Either they have boyfriends, or hangups, or they like girls. Whatever the reason, as a freshman you will have no girlfriend. If I knew why, I would not be alone.

—JOE MAYAN
CARNEGIE MELLON UNIVERSITY, SOPHOMORE

• • • • • • • •

DON'T DATE SOMEONE you're good friends with. If you go to a small school, it becomes a thing where everyone knows about your business, everyone knows everything about your relationship.

—CONOR MCNEIL
EMORY UNIVERSITY, SOPHOMORE

• • • • • • • •

NEVER TRY TO TWO-TIME ANYBODY, because you always get caught. Don't do that. Two-timing is bad; that's a tough lesson to learn. I was with this girl, and I didn't think it was serious, but she thought it was. Then I got with another girl and the first one found out from someone she knew. She confronted me, and I was in the dog house. But I talked my way back into the relationship, and that is hard to do. I learned my lesson: If you got someone, you better take care of her. College is a small world; smaller than you think. So respect the women.

—ANONYMOUS
BROWN UNIVERSITY, SOPHOMORE

• • • • • • • •

THE SINGLE-ROOM BATHROOMS in the college library are the best place to have quickie sex on campus.

—J.
UNIVERSITY OF GEORGIA, 1996

☆ **IT MAY LOOK LIKE THE GIRLS** who are out partying, and doing who knows what with who knows who, are the girls getting the guys. But they're not, really. Also, the nice boys are not on sports teams. I don't know where they are, but they're not on sports teams.

—*EBELE ONYEMA*
GEORGETOWN UNIVERSITY, SENIOR

• • • • • • • •

I LEFT A SERIOUS RELATIONSHIP hanging when I left high school, so I didn't date anyone seriously my whole freshman year. I just hooked up and had one-night stands. I enjoyed being single in college—true love will come eventually, and until then, you should have some fun.

—*P.*
PRINCETON UNIVERSITY, SOPHOMORE

• • • • • • • •

I'VE SEEN THE MISTAKE OF PEOPLE staying with their high-school boyfriend and girlfriend, then breaking up with them senior year. That's a terrible experience. You lose the entire novelty of being in college. I would recommend meeting new people and going out with different types of people, whether they're from other states or countries, or whatever.

—*MIKE*
UNIVERSITY OF TEXAS AT AUSTIN, 1995

• • • • • • • •

HOOKING UP—DON'T DO IT ON HALLOWEEN unless you really know who is behind that costume. I had a lot to drink and ended up with a very big surprise once we got comfortable. I ran out of there quickly: it was a very homely girl.

—*JAMIE JASTA*
CARNEGIE MELLON UNIVERSITY, SENIOR

When you're not paying attention, that's when someone will be looking at you.

—*SARAH*
GEORGIA INSTITUTE OF TECHNOLOGY
2002

MY SISTER IS A FRESHMAN. I told her not to hook up with a lot of guys, not to get a bad reputation, because you can't shake it; it follows you everywhere. I'm a senior now, and some of the people that in my opinion have had bad reputations for whatever reason, when I look at them now, that's what I think of. Some people have been away for a year, studying abroad; some people, I haven't seen them since freshman year. But the reputation sticks.

—*TIM JOYCE*
GEORGETOWN UNIVERSITY, SENIOR

• • • • • • • •

"Try to avoid feeling committed to anyone the first year. Don't get too serious about dating any particular person. Spend some time. And I wouldn't go in with too much baggage from high school, either."

—*RYAN A. BROWN*
UNIVERSITY OF NORTH CAROLINA AT CHAPEL HILL, 1998

• • • • • • • •

DON'T DO ANYTHING WITH A GIRL who's not making rational decisions; that's a good way to get thrown in jail. It's better to be extremely modest in that situation. If a girl wants to do something with you, you can do it the next time or three times down the road.

—*NICHOLAS BONAWITZ*
UNIVERSITY OF ROCHESTER, 2001

SADDER BUT WISER

I met my girlfriend in my freshman year. All year long I had been active with my dorm. It was coed and very community-oriented. Then my friend moved into my dorm, and things changed. We started dating and did the whole isolation thing, and it was especially dumb because of the community feeling on our floor. As it turned out, I dated her until spring of senior year, and in the process, I stopped really doing the whole college scene thing; this is something one should definitely not do.

Breaking up with my girlfriend was the hardest thing I have ever done: basically, you grow up with the person in college, and you go through your whole college experience with just them. I found myself almost at the beginning of the cycle; having to develop friends and cultivate relationships, and trying to bring back friendships with people I had deserted over the years.

—D.
AMERICAN UNIVERSITY, 1999

ASK PEOPLE OUT. It takes guts but you'll never know unless you try. And everyone appreciates a little more courtship and a little less of the senseless hookup culture.

—*SEAN CAMERON*
PRINCETON UNIVERSITY, SOPHOMORE

• • • • • • • •

I HAVE A FRIEND WHO STARTED DATING her boyfriend about a week after they got to college. She never really did freshman year like some people do, and it's affecting her now. She feels like she didn't go through the crazy freshman stuff before getting into a serious relationship.

—*HANNAH*
EMORY UNIVERSITY, JUNIOR

• • • • • • • •

I TRANSFERRED TO ANOTHER SCHOOL because my girlfriend couldn't get into my school. After I transferred there, we dated for another six months, then broke up. I felt like an idiot, because I had transferred to an easier school.

—*JUAN GONZALEZ*
CLEMSON UNIVERSITY, 1988

• • • • • • • •

DATING IS COOL. It's not a problem as long as the person you're dating doesn't try to keep you from doing what you have to do in school. If you have to study, if you have work to do and they're saying, let's go here and there, that might be a problem.

—*KEVIN L.*
GEORGIA INSTITUTE OF TECHNOLOGY, JUNIOR

• • • • • • • •

DON'T EVER HAVE A SERIOUS BOYFRIEND your first semester. You don't want to be known only as someone's girlfriend, and you also need time to figure out your own life.

—*LIANA METZGER*
MASSACHUSETTS INSTITUTE OF TECHNOLOGY, 2003

Avoid meeting people at frat parties when you're looking to date. It's hard to tell how sincere they are when you're a freshman.

—*ANN MALIPATIL*
EMORY UNIVERSITY
SENIOR

STAY AWAY FROM THE BOYS on the athletic teams; they're players in the dating scene. They think they're really cool, and they take advantage of the freshman girls. The freshmen girls come in and they're in awe, and the athletes hit on them and take advantage of them. Beware.

—*A.*
GEORGETOWN UNIVERSITY, SOPHOMORE

If you're looking for love, be patient.

—*KHALIL SULLIVAN*
PRINCETON UNIVERSITY, JUNIOR

• • • • • • • •

"Advice on dating: Don't. It costs too much. Go out with friends and meet new people. If you do date, don't date one person exclusively. It only leads to trouble."

—*JIMMY LYNCH*
AUBURN UNIVERSITY, 2001

• • • • • • • •

YOU DON'T EVER WANT TO MOVE IN with a girl-friend. If you do, your lifestyle becomes limited; you always have to come home with her and you always have to deal with her. I had roommates who were a couple living together in my house and I saw them fighting all the time. The reason was that they were together too much, and the expectations grow and grow and if they don't meet those expectations for one moment, they get in a fight.

—*STEPHAN*
UNIVERSITY OF CALIFORNIA AT SANTA BARBARA, 2002

YOU COME TO COLLEGE and there are women everywhere; that's probably the best thing about it. But you have to have your act together. If you don't have your obligations in order, you're never going to make it. I've seen people fail out of college in the first year. But if you have your time managed right, there's nothing you can't do.

—*CHRIS MCANDREW*
UNIVERSITY OF DELAWARE, JUNIOR

• • • • • • • •

❝My free time is spent maintaining my room and all my stuff and doing work, so there's very little time left for dates.❞

—*MATT MONACO*
GEORGE WASHINGTON UNIVERSITY, FRESHMAN

• • • • • • • •

HERE'S HOW THE IM THING WORKS with dating: You hang out with a bunch of friends and there's this one person you have an interest in and you want to improve that. It used to be that you would have to call them. Now the IM is an icebreaker. You ask for their IM name and you chat a little and get to know them. Then you call them.

—*CHRIS PROVENCHER*
JAMES MADISON UNIVERSITY, FRESHMAN

LATE-NIGHT HANGOUT: top of the parking deck at the medical center. Great views, quiet, good for making out. For the thrill factor: the 50-yard line in the football stadium.

—*MARGOT CARMICHAEL LESTER*
UNIVERSITY OF NORTH CAROLINA AT CHAPEL HILL, 1983

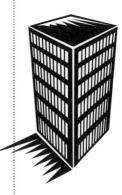

• • • • • • • •

MAKE SURE TO PRACTICE SAFE SEX. If you have a roommate, devise a code early on. We used to have a magnet on the door and if one of us had our girlfriend over we would flip the magnet upside down. I don't remember if this ever stopped us from "accidentally" walking in.

—*ANONYMOUS*
UNIVERSITY OF FLORIDA, 1993

• • • • • • • •

DON'T TRUST PEOPLE as quickly as you might want to. As a freshman girl, you could get in a lot of trouble if you don't watch yourself. Listen to your friends when they say you shouldn't do something. They probably know something more than you. You probably won't listen to them; but you should.

—*LAUREN*
GEORGETOWN UNIVERSITY, SOPHOMORE

• • • • • • • •

 I DIDN'T REALLY DATE. I went to clubs a lot; danced and partied, but all for fun. I gave guys fake phone numbers (that was fun). Just remember, dancing with a guy and going home with a guy are two different things. Kissing a guy at a club and going home with a guy are two different things. One thing does not always need to lead to the other. Be patient. And no, boys will not die if you don't "help them out."

—*LESLIE M.*
UNIVERSITY OF FLORIDA, 1995

With relationships, don't be afraid to wait. If you're a girl, there are so many guys.

—*LAURA MANNO*
GEORGIA INSTITUTE OF TECHNOLOGY SOPHOMORE

SEASONAL AFFECTION DISORDER

Take full advantage of all of the social opportunities that college offers a freshman, and avoid any serious relationships that may hamper or deter you from enjoying all of the rites of passage of being a college freshman. There is no better time than fall on a college campus, with fraternity/sorority rush, parties, and football games to enjoy and revel in. If you have a significant other, or meet someone who could quickly become a significant other, find any reason to put that relationship off until winter when it gets cold and the social life slows down a bit. Keep in mind however, that after winter comes spring break, when once again, all ties must be broken.

I learned this lesson the hard way; I had a serious girlfriend who attended Auburn while I was attending Georgia Tech. Not only did I put many unnecessary miles on my car, I also missed the opportunity to meet many other interesting coeds with a lot to offer. While my fraternity and college experience was certainly not without its share of fun, a serious long-distance girlfriend did not enhance it. And to make matters worse, I actually dropped a Naval ROTC scholarship (and an opportunity to become a pilot) after my freshman year because I thought I would rather marry the Auburn coed than cruise the Mediterranean on an aircraft carrier. Needless to say, we broke up less than a year after this very forward-looking decision. That's another reason for stalling those serious entangling relationships early in college; they hamper logical decision-making.

—*S.A.H.*
GEORGIA INSTITUTE OF TECHNOLOGY, 1987

USE REQUIRED P.E. CREDITS to your advantage in meeting potential dates. Girls, try bowling or weightlifting. Boys, go with ballroom dancing or walking.

—*WENDY W.*
UNIVERSITY OF GEORGIA, 1996

• • • • • • • •

✓ **GUYS LIE. STAY AWAY FROM SPORTS PLAYERS,** because they lie. I dated a baseball player; I really liked him a lot. Then all of a sudden people started coming up to me and asking me if I was pregnant. He was going around telling everybody that I was pregnant! I was like, "How do I not know that I am pregnant and you're going around telling everyone that I am?" Become friends with someone before you decide to get into a relationship. Now I date someone from back home. College relationships do not work.

—*SWEETS*
GEORGIA STATE UNIVERSITY, JUNIOR

• • • • • • • •

THE SUMMER AFTER MY FRESHMAN YEAR, I met this guy who lived hundreds of miles from my school. We dated for a year and a half: I drove to his town, five hours away, almost every single weekend of my sophomore year; it really got old. Long-distance relationships suck. Don't try it.

There are a lot of scumbags out there who try to take advantage of girls, especially freshmen. Don't put your drink down or let someone else get you a drink, because they could put something in it. Never walk around campus alone at night. Be careful.

—*KATHERINE*
AUBURN UNIVERSITY, 2001

Guys, be aggressive meeting girls. It's not going to come to you. You've got to make it happen yourself.

—*ALEC*
BOSTON COLLEGE JUNIOR

DON'T DATE SOMEONE IN YOUR HALLWAY; I did. Not only are you living together, but you also have shared counselors and shared activities; you can't escape them. Anytime I went anywhere, or anytime he went anywhere, we would know about it. We'd have fights over IM, and sometimes we'd have to run down the hallway to go yell at each other. And even if we were to break up, there was no chance of having our own lives without the other person knowing about it. So I basically continued to date him for the whole year, regardless of how happy I was, in order to not deal with the issues involved with having him around.

—*CATE*
BROWN UNIVERSITY, JUNIOR

• • • • • • • •

IF YOU'RE TALKING TO SOMEONE at a party and you hit it off, an easy way to talk to them again and not wait for the next party, is to ask him if he wants to IM. You can tell him that you're so addicted to IM; make a joke about it. Get his screen name; I've done that.

—*EDITH ZIMMERMAN*
WESLEYAN UNIVERSITY, SOPHOMORE

TOP 5
COED-BUT-MOSTLY-FEMALE SCHOOLS

1. Parsons School of Design   (75% female)
2. Sarah Lawrence College   (73%)
3. Adelphi University   (71%)
4. Bennington College   (70%)
5. Goucher College   (70%)

MY SISTER CAME TO MY SCHOOL, and I had all my friends make sure she didn't hook up with anyone. The thing I told her was to get wasted a lot; it's needed.

—*JOEL*
PRINCETON UNIVERSITY, 2002

• • • • • • • •

I HAD A BOYFRIEND AT HOME when I left for freshman year. That was much more traumatic than leaving my parents behind. I know a lot of people who did that, especially at an all-girls school. Everyone came with boyfriends, but by the middle of the year they weren't with them anymore.

—*LAUREN WEBSTER*
BARNARD COLLEGE, JUNIOR

• • • • • • • •

DON'T DATE PEOPLE IN YOUR DORM, especially if you're just hooking up after a party, because there will be a break-up and, therefore, awkwardness in the dorm. It's impossible to avoid someone in your building. You'll step into the elevator and they'll be there and everything gets silent.

—*REID ATTAWAY*
JAMES MADISON UNIVERSITY, FRESHMAN

Advice to the guys—know that she's just waiting for you to come up to her and say hi. I'm now in grad school; it took me 7 years to figure that out.

—*KAMAL FREIHA*
UNIVERSITY OF OREGON, 1997

TOP 5
COED-BUT-MOSTLY-MALE SCHOOLS

1. United States Naval Academy   (85% male)
2. United States Air Force Academy   (84%)
3. United States Military Academy   (84%)
4. Rose-Hulman Institute of Technology   (80%)
5. Worcester Polytechnic Institute   (77%)

DO NOT HAVE SEXUAL RELATIONS WITH ANYONE IN your dorm, because if you have a one-night stand, you don't necessarily want to see them the next day; that creates tension. Dating isn't a bad idea; it just depends on whether you can handle a relationship. I recommend dating; it's healthy.

—*N.*
EMORY UNIVERSITY, JUNIOR

• • • • • • • •

Don't be afraid to be alone; take a class, meet strangers, join a club by yourself.

—*WENDY W.*
UNIVERSITY OF GEORGIA, 1996

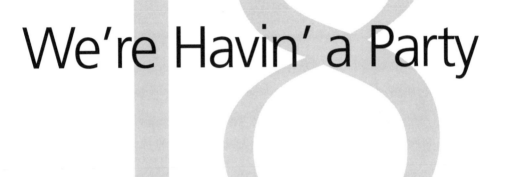

We're Havin' a Party

The party scene in college may be a lot like your high school, but at the end of the night Mom and Dad won't be waiting up to check you out. It's all your call now. Here's some detailed advice from the veterans about when to party, how to drink or how not to, and all the rest.

IF YOU WANT TO DRINK FOR FREE, head to a bar and pretend you don't want to drink alcohol. You'll suddenly be everyone's pet project. As the efforts to convert you mount, give in slowly; not only will everyone have a good time, but you'll have a good buzz to match.

—*BRIAN TURNER*
UNIVERSITY OF GEORGIA, 1996

DON'T PARTY BEFORE TESTS. IT REALLY DOES IMPAIR YOUR ABILITY.

—*H.K.S.*
OXFORD COLLEGE JUNIOR

HOW TO SURVIVE YOUR FRESHMAN YEAR

Don't drink the punch. There's a lot more alcohol in there than you think.

—*Anonymous*
Yale University
Sophomore

Now you're out on your own. Just because you can sleep with every woman and do every drug and drink everything, it doesn't mean you have to or you should. It'll take you a while to figure that out.

—*A.W.D.*
Georgia State University, 1987

• • • • • • • •

If you're going to drink, get to know your bartender personally. Big tipping, right off the bat, is a good way to do this.

—*J.G.*
Florida State University, 1991

• • • • • • • •

If you're going to drink, drink *before* you go out. It saves tons of money. Use the money you save to buy an Xbox or Playstation to keep you occupied.

—*Jimmy Lynch*
Auburn University, 2001

• • • • • • • •

I smoked a lot of pot; that was something entertaining that came with college. I had smoked before, but not to the extent I did my first year, which could very likely be a reason it is so unmemorable.

—*K.*
San Diego State University, Junior

• • • • • • • •

Don't drink liquor—stick to beer. You have better control with beer. I had bad experiences with liquor. If you wake up the next morning and you don't remember what you did, you've had too much to drink.

—*Reid Attaway*
James Madison University, Freshman

IF YOU'VE NEVER FUNNELED THREE BEERS after going shot for shot with some guy in your Bio lab, don't do it the first night on campus; you will end up throwing up in the washrooms, and it is just not pretty. Yes, college is a time for experimentation and partying, but don't screw up what you worked twelve years for just because the opportunity is there.

> —*AMY*
> *PRINCETON UNIVERSITY, FRESHMAN*

• • • • • • • •

GO TO PARTIES. I didn't party at all in high school. When I went to college, my R.A. took me to a frat party the second night I was there. I wouldn't say overdo it, but you should experience that part of college life.

> —*ERIC FRIES*
> *BOSTON UNIVERSITY, 1997*

No matter how desperate you are for a daiquiri, do not use blueberries.

> —*MARGOT*
> *CARMICHAEL LESTER*
> *UNIVERSITY OF*
> *NORTH CAROLINA*
> *AT CHAPEL HILL*
> *1983*

• • • • • • • •

"Don't try to drink all the beer on campus. You can't, trust me. And not having a car your freshman year is a good safety measure."

> —*STEVE DAVIS*
> *FLORIDA STATE UNIVERSITY, 1988*

• • • • • • • •

IF A MAN APPROACHES YOU and your friends at a garden party offering strange-looking mushrooms in a baggie, tell him you're not hungry.

> —*D.D.*
> *UNIVERSITY OF PENNSYLVANIA, 1989*

FRESHMAN DRINKING PRIMER

1) EVERY COLLEGE STUDENT NEEDS TO KNOW the old mantra, "Liquor before beer, never fear. Beer before liquor, never sicker."

2) IT HELPS TO HAVE A GLASS OF WATER WITH, or in between, drinks. And don't drink on an empty stomach.

3) IF YOU CLOSE YOUR EYES and you can't keep your balance, it's probably time to stop drinking for the night.

> —D.R.
> UNIVERSITY OF NORTH CAROLINA AT CHAPEL HILL, 1991

• • • • • • • •

TO PREVENT SERIOUS TROUBLE—and perhaps even death—you must follow some simple rules. First of all, you need to do the stand-up test: The first time you drink a lot of liquor, don't do it all sitting down. You won't feel what it's doing to you. But the first time you stand up, hit the floor, and eat some carpet, you will suddenly feel what it is doing to you. So, stand up often while in the process of drinking liquor, to better measure the effect. Also, drink a lot of water when drinking alcohol; you've got to dilute that stuff.

> —R.S.
> GEORGETOWN UNIVERSITY, 1990

• • • • • • • •

THE BEST WAY TO GET OVER A HANGOVER is water and bread. Bread is your best friend: It helps take care of your stomach, and it fills you and soaks up anything. The water makes you not dehydrated any more. The next day, just make it a Blockbuster night; that's all you need to do.

> —BETH
> DIABLO VALLEY COLLEGE, FRESHMAN

FOOTBALL GAMES ARE SO MUCH FUN HERE—everyone is drunk in the stands. On game day, the whole campus is up by 9 a.m. You can't get students up at 9 a.m. for school, but they'll get up early to start partying before a game.

> —*M.M.*
> BOSTON COLLEGE, JUNIOR

• • • • • • • •

" If you're a bunch of girls and you go to a frat party, which you will, be aware of your surroundings and keep track of each other. Be in charge of yourself, and keep track of your girls, and they'll keep track of you. "

> —*TRACY*
> UNIVERSITY OF COLORADO, 2001

• • • • • • • •

ALCOHOL IS A REALLY BIG FACTOR in what goes wrong with freshmen. Everything is new, you're getting a lot of attention from other people, and when you're under the influence of alcohol you don't make the best decisions. And there's peer pressure: A lot of people think they're above peer pressure, but when you get in a scene with a hundred other people having a good time, you don't do things you would normally do.

> —*A.G.H.*
> UNIVERSITY OF VIRGINIA, SENIOR

Go to places with free beer.

> —*JOEL*
> PRINCETON
> UNIVERSITY, 2002

AS FAR AS DRINKING GOES, I had a closed mind. I thought, I don't want to go through four years of school drunk and not experiencing everything. I didn't realize you could balance those things. So I didn't drink at all. Then I gradually started with friends here and I was like, you know what? Going out with friends on Friday night and partying doesn't mean you're wasting four years. It just means you're experiencing different things.

—*LYNN SNIFFEN*
BOSTON COLLEGE, JUNIOR

• • • • • • • •

"Alcohol makes some people seem more attractive than they will look the next morning. So, think a little more about your decisions at frat parties or anything like that."

—*H.K.S.*
OXFORD COLLEGE, JUNIOR

• • • • • • • •

Stay on top of your stuff, and regulate your drinking habits.

—*BRETT STRICKLAND*
GEORGIA STATE
UNIVERSITY
FRESHMAN

I TRANSFERRED FROM a tremendous party school. I wasn't disciplined to study when I first got to school—and Chico breeds that: you never want to miss a party or a band playing. There are too many things going on; it's difficult to pace yourself. So I'm pleased with my transfer to a smaller school; I enjoy school more and appreciate my free time, because I've earned it after completing my studies.

—*TOM CHRISTENSEN*
DOMINICAN UNIVERSITY, SENIOR

☆ **YOU END UP IN PRETTY WEIRD SITUATIONS.**
Once I went to a party of all Indians. Everyone in the room was Indian except me. The food, the conversations, the dress—everything was Indian. By the end of the night I thought I was Indian and was ready to give up beef forever.

—*JOE MAYAN*
CARNEGIE MELLON UNIVERSITY, SOPHOMORE

• • • • • • • •

I DON'T DRINK. It's not hard to socialize if you don't drink, because everyone needs a designated driver. If I go, they usually buy my dinner. So it works for me.

—*B.M.*
UNIVERSITY OF MARYLAND, JUNIOR

• • • • • • • •

IN HIS FRESHMAN YEAR, my roommate smoked pot for the first time. At the end of his freshman year, he dropped out of school, moved back in with his mom, learned how to be a DJ, and now spends his days smoking more pot and playing Dungeons & Dragons with the other pot smokers he meets at the local coffee shops.

—*STEVEN COY*
SAN DIEGO STATE, SOPHOMORE

• • • • • • • •

✓ **DON'T FEEL LIKE YOU NEED** to funnel beers to have a good time, and know that if you choose not to drink, there are tons of other people who don't either. But don't lecture other people— if they wanted you to be their mom, they would've asked. Exceptions: your close friends, people who are being offensive to you, people you are close to, and girls who are about to be taken advantage of because of their state.

—*JULIE*
PRINCETON UNIVERSITY, SOPHOMORE

☆ If you're going to buy weed, don't buy it from the drunk on the street. What you'll end up with is oregano held together by glue.

—*J.G.*
FLORIDA STATE UNIVERSITY, 1991

HERE'S SOME ADVICE that my brother left me on my answering machine the first week I was in college: "If you smoke pot in your room, make sure to put a towel under the door."

—*B.K.*
CORNELL UNIVERSITY, 1996

• • • • • • • •

I DON'T DRINK. When I go to parties, people ask why I'm not drinking and I'll just tell them I decided I don't want to do it. Ninety percent of the people I talk to about it—even the people who are completely drunk—think it's cool and say I should stick with it.

—*REID ATTAWAY*
JAMES MADISON UNIVERSITY, FRESHMAN

• • • • • • • •

At parties, never set a drink down and walk away.

—*SWEETS*
GEORGIA STATE UNIVERSITY, JUNIOR

NEVER EVER DRIVE AFTER DRINKING ANY AMOUNT of alcohol at all. A DUI will give you a police record and cost you thousands in legal fees and fines; don't even chance it. I had friends who did, and once it happens, all you can do is regret what you've done.

Be wary of hard liquor. Don't drink it or let others guzzle it like weak beer. That can easily be a quick slide to alcohol poisoning, coma—even death.

—*WENDY W.*
UNIVERSITY OF GEORGIA, 1996

• • • • • • • •

I DON'T PARTY A LOT NOW. The first couple of years, I partied too much. I realized, this is a lot of work, trying to party and go to school, and it's expensive. So, I decided I didn't need it; it's too much effort.

—*ADAM PENA*
AMERICAN REPERTORY THEATER AT HARVARD, JUNIOR

WISDOM FOR WOMEN

When you go out, have someone with you that you trust—I don't care if you're just going over to a guy's house, you don't want to be left alone. You need a friend who knows when to take you home. I have a friend and we do that for each other; we don't let each other out of sight. Sometimes I'll get pissed off and get in a full-on fist fight, saying, "No, I can handle this!" and she's like, "No, I'm taking you home right now." We have to be strict with each other, but it's good to have someone looking out for you.

The best place to hide from guys is in the bathroom. Just make puking noises and they'll run. That's all you have to do to be left alone.

I don't care where you go to school, you have to be tough; two girls were raped in my dorm. Take a kickboxing class so that you know you can protect yourself.

> —MOLLY SELMER
> SONOMA STATE UNIVERSITY, 2002

• • • • • • • •

When you're drinking, know your limits. Girls don't know how much they can drink, because they don't drink as often as guys. So girls will play drinking games with guys, thinking that they're cool and tough; then all of a sudden they're messed up, throwing up, or passed out.

> —JENNIFER SPICER
> FOOTHILL COLLEGE, 2000

YOU'RE GOING TOO FAR with the drinking when you have to drink every time you want to go out. When you "pre-game" for everything: "Let's go to the diner, let's pre-game first!"—that kind of thing. Some people have an obsession with it.

Don't become an alcoholic; that screws up everything. I've seen people screw up their whole school career. They do too many drugs or drink too much, they're not in school anymore, and they're working hard to get back in.

—*DANIEL RUSK*
UNIVERSITY OF MARYLAND, SOPHOMORE

• • • • • • • •

"I worked in the bars on the weekends, which was cool because you're still in the social scene and you can see everyone, but you're making money instead of spending money."

—*STEVEN RILEY*
STATE UNIVERSITY OF NEW YORK AT BINGHAMTON, 1993

• • • • • • • •

DON'T DRINK TOO MUCH; at this school, it can cost you a lot of money. My freshman year, my roommate got alcohol poisoning. She came home early one morning and passed out. We couldn't wake her up so we called campus security and an ambulance came and took her to the hospital. She was fine afterwards, but the school fined her $2000; plus, she had to pay her hospital bill.

—*LIANA HIYANE*
SANTA CLARA UNIVERSITY, JUNIOR

ALWAYS PUT YOUR HAND over your drink, to keep people from putting something in your drink. Obviously, you shouldn't just leave your drink and come back to it. But also, cover your drink when you carry it. That was the overwhelming advice I got from everybody when I came to college.

> —BETHANY
> JAMES MADISON UNIVERSITY, SENIOR

• • • • • • • •

I DRANK AN UNGODLY AMOUNT OF BEER, smoked way too much pot, and took hallucinogens. That was the D-Chi way—and that's how I survived Union!

> —CHIEF
> UNION COLLEGE, 1990

• • • • • • • •

☆ **DON'T GET TOO CAUGHT UP IN ALCOHOL.** I personally believe that college is the time to experiment with stuff like this; but if you do plan on getting drunk, try to set a reasonable limit and abide by it. If you pace yourself, this isn't too hard to do. And definitely try to confine it to the weekend. If you start drinking Thursday or even Wednesday nights, your studies and your grades will suffer. There's nothing like coming home inebriated at 2 a.m. and still having homework to do for the next day, especially when your responsible friends already did it together as a group and have gone to sleep.

> —ANONYMOUS
> UNIVERSITY OF VIRGINIA, SENIOR

• • • • • • • •

GIRLS, BE ESPECIALLY CAREFUL of what you drink while at clubs or house parties, because an uncovered drink could mean a lost night and a trip to the gynecologist the next day.

> —ANONYMOUS

How can you tell if you're partying too much? If you're doing fine in classes, you're not partying too much. If you don't do well in classes, you're partying too much.

> —NOURA BAKKOUR
> GEORGETOWN
> UNIVERSITY
> SENIOR

TRY TO LIMIT THE DRINKING to three times a week. Work hard Monday through Thursday, and party Thursday, Friday, and Saturday nights; that's what worked for me.

—*NICK DOMANICO*
UNIVERSITY OF CALIFORNIA AT SANTA BARBARA, SENIOR

● ● ● ● ● ● ● ●

TRY TO STEER CLEAR OF THE DRINKING as much as possible. It's easy to get too fixed on the drinking of beers each night. That usually ends up causing trouble.

—*DAVID BLANEY*
WILLIAMS COLLEGE, 1985

● ● ● ● ● ● ● ●

❝Don't be a fool and party and act like an idiot. That happened to a bunch of girls on my hall and they all did poorly.❞

—*ERICA MARIOLA*
EMORY UNIVERSITY, 2002

● ● ● ● ● ● ● ●

I WENT TO A SMALL, JESUIT COLLEGE, but it was pretty cool. We had crazy frats and sororities, because we had a wet campus. I think a wet campus is good; you learn responsibility. If you hadn't had a drink before, it was very supportive. A lot of people knew what they were doing and helped the people who didn't. Every party we ever had was bussed; no one ever drove to parties or to go out. If you drove to go out, you drove because you were stupid.

—*GINGER M. BRODTMAN*
SPRING HILL COLLEGE, 1998

GO TO FRAT PARTIES with a bunch of girlfriends, and make sure you all go home together. Don't listen to any of the crap the guys try to hand you. They're looking for freshmen; they're waiting for them. Freshmen are so naïve and gullible and they think everything the guys say is true, and it's not. The guy will say anything: he'll say all these nice things and make a girl feel special, but it doesn't matter. He won't know your name the next day. He probably doesn't know your name right then.

—*KRISTIN THOMAS*
JAMES MADISON UNIVERSITY, JUNIOR

• • • • • • • •

STAND BY YOUR DRUNK FRIENDS

One of my girlfriends was really injury-prone. She would hurt herself constantly, usually while drinking. She almost died three or four times. One night we were out at a strip of bars and we got really drunk. She was standing like 30 feet away from me at the end of the street, and I'm standing with five people. She called my name and I saw her running towards me. Then, she's like sprinting at me. She gets like five feet from me and leaps at me—she wanted me to catch her, or something. I sidestepped her and she met the concrete. Her entire face was bruised and cut and it was Parents Week next weekend and everyone thought her boyfriend did it to her. Our  guy friends almost beat him up. She was called Scarface from that point on. The moral of the story is, don't sidestep your friends. Break their fall or something. But I blame the alcohol.

—*CASEY*
GEORGETOWN UNIVERSITY, SENIOR

MORE WISE WOMEN

There were a lot of freshman girls that I took home from bars; they thought they had friends. They got too drunk, and their friends left. We used to find girls drunk in the bathrooms of bars all the time. They didn't know where their friends were and they would need someone to take care of them.

Girls, don't put down your drink. I think I went to a great school, but you don't know who is around. I had a friend who was drugged her sophomore year. She had two beers and all of a sudden she's out of her head and can't stand. And we thought she must have done shots and we didn't know about it. But the next day, she was in bed and couldn't get up. And she'd had hardly anything to drink. You don't know who's out there; you have to be careful.

You don't want to go to bars when you're a freshman, anyway. You're not going to meet anyone that you want to meet. I mean, who do you meet at a bar? Alcoholics and weirdos.

> —J. DEVEREUX
> GEORGETOWN UNIVERSITY, 2002

• • • • • • • • •

You have to be careful. We went to frat parties where they kept trying to give us drinks and beers. They went into the bathroom and then came out with a cup of beer. We were like, "Wow, no. Can I watch you pour it, please?" Some girls don't know better.

> —CHRISTINE
> UNIVERSITY OF RHODE ISLAND, SOPHOMORE

IF YOU GET DRUNK, don't throw chairs at your dorm neighbor. My neighbor had the same major as mine and I saw her for the next four years. She remembered that.

—*CASEY*
GEORGETOWN UNIVERSITY, SENIOR

• • • • • • • •

"Don't drink to get drunk. You're not cool if you're drunk. Better to get a social buzz that keeps you in a jovial and rhythmic mood all night."

—*RICHARD*
GEORGIA SOUTHERN UNIVERSITY, 1992

• • • • • • • •

I DID SOME DUMB THINGS and I'm still paying for them. I did something illegal that I got caught for. Looking back now, I wish I could change some of the partying to more studying.

Don't get stupid; people remember that. People will say, "Oh, I remember that party when you were passed out on the stairs." Whatever you do, it will follow you around the rest of your life. You want to have a good time, but you don't want to get carried away.

Everyone does stupid things, but don't get caught doing something illegal. You pick up habits in your freshman year where you say, "Oh, I didn't get caught then, so I might as well do it now." Then you get caught, and you're like, "Oh, that's how the real world works."

—*JOSH H.*
PURDUE UNIVERSITY, 1998

Just because the beer is being served in Dixie cups doesn't mean you can drink 40 cups and still drive home.

—*SCOTT WOELFEL*
UNIVERSITY OF MISSOURI, 1981

DON'T TAKE ECSTASY. The younger generations take it too much. I took this class, "The Legal Approach to Drugs and Alcohol Abuse." In the 70's people abused acid, in the 80's it was cocaine, and late 90's until now younger people abuse ecstasy. It's bad for you, and it can be mixed with other substances. Don't do it.

—*STEPHAN*
UNIVERSITY OF CALIFORNIA AT SANTA BARBARA, 2002

66 Don't feel that you need to be at every party all the time. It's perfectly OK to be at home sleeping on a Saturday night; there's nothing wrong with that. More people do it than you think. If you get too caught up in the social scene, you lose sight of other things. 99

—*HANNAH SMITH*
HARVARD UNIVERSITY, JUNIOR

THERE WAS A LOT OF VOMITING in freshman year—something to avoid. My one rule is, never clean up anyone else's vomit. But that also means that when you vomit, you have to expect to clean it up by yourself.

—*CAITLIN BERBERICH*
UNIVERSITY OF GEORGIA, 2001

WORDS OF WARNING

Don't make drinking a competitive activity. If you find yourself trying to prove how much you can drink to impress others, then it's going to end badly. You'll get alcohol poisoning, whether you believe you're immune or not. Or, you'll end up puking your guts out in front of your friends and people you don't even know. Also, drinking should not be the main activity of your night. If you go out just to drink, you're going to get drunk. If you go out to meet people at a party, or to dance, play a game, or bowl, focus on the main activity first, and then just let the drinking be an additive; it should never be the focus of your night. The funny thing is, the people who make it the focus of their night can't understand why everyone else might not want to do the same thing. But watch those people; they're all cool and everything when they're playing quarters and making jokes and doing shots, but they'll end up puking or acting like idiots.

—*ANONYMOUS*
VILLANOVA, 2001

• • • • • • • • •

If you do decide to experiment with alcohol and drugs in college, be prepared to accept the consequences of your actions; what you're doing may be illegal and, as such, a poor decision. Alcohol and drugs are only a temporary escape from the dullness of life. If you find yourself consumed by these substances, you may need to re-evaluate the directions your life is going in and realign yourself. If you're drinking to be more social, then maybe you're too self-conscious. If you're smoking marijuana to relax and be happy, then maybe you need a hobby. There are plenty of people and activities on campus to keep you busy without having to resort to drugs and alcohol on too regular a basis.

—*ARIEL MELENDEZ*
PRINCETON UNIVERSITY, FRESHMAN

I WENT TO SCHOOL ABOUT THREE HOURS from the Mexican border. My freshman year, I was kind of an idiot. I went down to Mexico, and coming back across the border, I had had a few beers. Well, they stop you and ask if you have anything to declare. So I said, "Nothing to declare, except for my automatic weapons." It was a joke, but it wasn't taken well by the border patrol. A couple of hours later, after being strip-searched and interrogated, I was told never to come into the country again.

—*JOHN BENTLEY*
TRINITY UNIVERSITY, 1995

IN MY FRESHMAN YEAR I would go out every night on weeknights and stay out until 5 a.m., when I had to be in class at 9 a.m. I wasn't making it. That was the last semester I didn't live at home.

—*ODELL*
HUNTER COLLEGE, SENIOR

YOU HAVE TO LEARN that the week is for studying and the weekend is for partying. You can't think that you just party every day. That's what I thought: I thought that college was a never-ending party, without work. I thought it was going to be easier than high school, without busy work. But it's overwhelming.

—*AMY HOFFBERG*
UNIVERSITY OF DELAWARE, FRESHMAN

IF YOU DON'T WANT TO DRINK, then it's all about the people you find. If you surround yourself with people who drink and who will pressure you, it will be a difficult situation. If you surround yourself with people who are hesitant to drink or who are responsible, it won't be such a problem.

—*ANONYMOUS*
UNIVERSITY OF VIRGINIA, SENIOR

BE RESPONSIBLE FOR YOUR FRIENDS. Make your own drinks. Watch where your friends are at all times. Don't be naïve about guys; know that they don't have your best interests in mind. I know several girls who were very trusting and were taken advantage of. It's really easy to do when everyone is under the influence of alcohol.

—A.G.H.
UNIVERSITY OF VIRGINIA, SENIOR

• • • • • • • •

DRINKING: I GOT WRITTEN UP BY THE POLICE multiple times for stupid reasons. It caused me some problems with housing for my sophomore year. And I lost housing for my senior year. I'm pretty liberal about drinking, but you've got to watch yourself. Blackouts are never too good.

—M.M.
BOSTON COLLEGE, JUNIOR

• • • • • • • •

✔ **A FRESHMAN GUY FINDS A GOOD PARTY** by finding some hot freshman girls and going where they go. Or, you can hook up with an upperclassman; they know where the good parties are.

—DAVE
UNIVERSITY OF RHODE ISLAND, JUNIOR

• • • • • • • •

YOU KNOW YOU'RE AT A GOOD PARTY when you get slammed against the wall trying to get to the keg in the corner. And guys try to get girls to go in for them. Girls get alcohol more easily than guys do.

—WHITNEY
YALE UNIVERSITY, FRESHMAN

BEST PARTY SCHOOLS

University of Colorado at Boulder

University of Wisconsin-Madison

Indiana University-Bloomington

University of Illinois at Urbana-Champaign

Washington and Lee University (Virginia)

FRESHMAN FACTOID

44 percent of college students "binge drink" (defined as drinking at least 5 [for men] or 4 [for women] drinks in a row, at least once in the previous two weeks). Last year 1,400 college students in the United States died in alcohol-related deaths.

WHEN YOU FIRST START COLLEGE, the phrase "three-day weekend" takes on a whole new meaning. The more social students tend to go out on Thursday night for the sole purpose of drinking themselves into a stupor. Friday night is a rest-and-recuperation night, and then the partying resumes Saturday night. By the time you wake up on Sunday it's already mid-afternoon. This trend fades by the time you start sophomore year. If it doesn't, you are officially an alcoholic and/or a stoner.

—JOSHUA BERKOV
BROWN UNIVERSITY, JUNIOR

. . . .

ALWAYS GO TO PARTIES with people you know, and be careful with your alcohol, wherever you put it down. And don't drink so much, because there are cops around. And don't do anything stupid, if you can help it. And don't run across the busy street, and don't be stupid in front of cops, and don't drive drunk. But have fun.

—ANONYMOUS
JAMES MADISON UNIVERSITY, SOPHOMORE

. . . .

THE FIRST WEEK OF SCHOOL, I WENT OUT partying with my friends and next thing I remember, I was locked outside my room with no key, naked and soaking wet at 5 in the morning.

—S.
HARVARD UNIVERSITY, SOPHOMORE

. . . .

WHEN YOU'RE AT A PARTY, TRY TO THINK about the next morning. Ask yourself the question: Will I be able to look at myself in the mirror?

—G.
UNIVERSITY OF NORTH CAROLINA AT CHAPEL HILL, SOPHOMORE

SCARY STORY

It was Halloween of my freshman year. We were having a party in the dorm—not a costume deal or anything, just partying in random rooms. I was drinking mainly screwdrivers out of one of those 42-ounce, McDonald's cups. A friend of a friend, who came up to visit with her meathead boyfriend, got into a fight with him and ran away. She was about to get us written up—at Westfield State, "written up" means getting kicked off campus for five weekends—so my friend and I split up to find her. I found the psycho tucked under a stairwell, crying. I put my hand out to help her up, and the crazy girl bit me really hard. The mark she left looked like ringworm!

I said, "Whatever," gave up on that problem, and proceeded to get fizzled for rizzle—drunk, that is. The vodka I was drinking was good old Poland Springs vodka, the cheapest form of the stuff around. Let's just say that at the end of the night I puked in my roommate's garbage and passed out face down on my rug. It does not end there: I woke up outside, crying, to the sound of a fire alarm. My friends told me they had come into my room, where I was just walking around in circles; they put my jacket on me and brought me outside. This is where I allegedly was crying to call my mother. Fortunately, I don't think that many people saw my scene. Anyway, my friends ended up bringing me to my other friend's dorm and putting me to sleep. That is what I like to call Alcoholism.

Lessons learned: 1) Screw your friend who is about to get written up, and 2) Drink beer—it could save your life.

—B.
WESTFIELD STATE COLLEGE, 2002

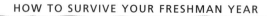

GRADUATION REQUIREMENT

If the smoke doesn't get you, the exhaustion will: During homecoming weekend at Dartmouth, the graduating class does a Senior Sweep—running around a 70-story bonfire in the center of the green. The class of 2004 has to circle it 104 times, the class of 2005, 105 times, and so on.

• • • • • • • •

A LOT OF PEOPLE COME IN HERE and they don't have experience drinking, and they just sort of explode. My friend had a freshman roommate who failed out the first semester because he had spent all his time drinking. Don't get in over your head.

—LEE ROBERTS
UNIVERSITY OF NORTH CAROLINA AT CHAPEL HILL, SENIOR

Animal House: Fraternities and Sororities

W*hat's the truth about Greek life? How can you know as a freshman if it's right for you? Adjusting to college is enough of a challenge; now there's rushing and pledging and a funny-looking alphabet to learn. Our correspondents weigh in on this first-year quandary.*

I JOINED A FRAT THE SPRING SEMESTER of my freshman year. It was a great experience; the best thing I ever did. I was against fraternities completely, but I joined because my friend wanted me to get some wings with him. I got dragged into it, and now the brothers are my best friends. I was that guy who said, "Frat guys suck!" But things change.

—CHRIS MCANDREW
UNIVERSITY OF DELAWARE, JUNIOR

IF YOU DECIDE TO RUSH, TAKE THE WHOLE EXPERIENCE WITH A GRAIN OF SALT.

—D.
DUKE UNIVERSITY
SENIOR

BE SWEET AS PIE during your sorority pledge period and wait until after you're active to tell off the snots who were mean to you. Better yet, just steal their boyfriends.

—*LYNN LAMOUSIN*
LOUISIANA STATE UNIVERSITY, 1988

• • • • • • • •

I WENT TO A LARGE SCHOOL where you didn't have to be Greek to have a life. But I wanted both, so during my sophomore year I decided to pledge. This gave me time to make other friendships with people who weren't necessarily going Greek. And as it turned out, not all of my closest friends from freshman year decided to go Greek. My advice: Don't jump into pledging. Get to know the campus, get to know friends outside of Greek life, and get used to what life is like without it. That way you can decide if it's right for you. At my school, sororities were very competitive, and many women never got invited to join any sorority. So this was tough for some people.

—*ANONYMOUS*
INDIANA UNIVERSITY, 1995

• • • • • • • •

FRESHMAN GIRLS SHOULD GO through sorority Rush, but don't take it too seriously. If you take it to heart, people can tell. You run the risk of getting really hurt. It's just a group of girls; there are other things in life.

—*ANONYMOUS*
UNIVERSITY OF VIRGINIA, SOPHOMORE

• • • • • • • •

JOIN WHATEVER FRATERNITY ATTRACTS THE HOTTEST chicks—that's all frats are good for, anyway.

—*J.G.*
FLORIDA STATE UNIVERSITY, 1991

Even if you don't want to be in a frat, you should do Rush; you'll get free drinks and have fun.

—*J.D.*
EMORY UNIVERSITY SENIOR

THE STUFF YOU HEAR about wild frat hazing is mostly college lore; in fact, some of the pranks or "rituals" are most likely obsolete. Like, you hear about the "ookie cookie" or "splewie," but again, it's a myth—it's not all like *Animal House*.

—*JAMES WILLIS*
UNIVERSITY OF CALIFORNIA AT DAVIS, SENIOR

• • • • • • • •

❝❝At least try Rush. You don't have to pledge, but going through Rush is a really good time to meet other girls who are going through what you're going through. It's a really great bonding time.❞❞

—*DENISE O.*
UNION COLLEGE, JUNIOR

• • • • • • • •

I'M IN A SORORITY, and it's the best thing I've ever done in my life. I'm such a better person for being in a sorority. But it's way too early to pledge freshman year; I pledged sophomore year. You need to establish yourself at your college first. You meet your freshman group of friends; then you can pledge sophomore year. I did, and I didn't feel like I was pledging too late. The year I pledged, there were 450 sophomores, versus like 50 freshmen. It's just too much for freshmen.

—*KRISTIN THOMAS*
JAMES MADISON UNIVERSITY, JUNIOR

Don't bother going to frat parties. It's a bunch of stupid people who are drunk, and there are too many of them.

—*ROBIN JALEEL*
EMORY UNIVERSITY
2002

THE FIRST FRAT PARTY I went to as a pledge, they told us not to wear anything nice. First thing that happens when I walk in, a girl throws an entire beer on me. It was called Beer Splash. I was like, "This is where I want to be."

—*A.G.S.*
UNIVERSITY OF TENNESSEE, DID NOT GRADUATE

· · · · · · · ·

I WOULD RECOMMEND NOT JOINING A FRAT or sorority. I'm not a fan. I think it breeds uniformity and it's not intelligent.

—*ANONYMOUS*
YALE UNIVERSITY, SOPHOMORE

· · · · · · · ·

THE WHOLE PROCESS TRULY IS SUPERFICIAL. Sorority members judge rushies based slightly on appearance and primarily on a five- to ten-minute conversation that takes place within the most fake and uncomfortable environment. With all this in mind, if you want to join a sorority, you take it for what it is. Don't go into Rush believing that the girls you meet have the final say (or any say, for that matter) on who you are, or how "cool" or desirable you are. They're judging you based on a glimpse of who they think you are.

—*D.*
DUKE UNIVERSITY, SENIOR

· · · · · · · ·

I DID NOT JOIN A FRAT because I did not want to do chores. I did chores at home and left that behind; who needs it? But to meet girls, the frat guys do have an advantage.

—*INSU CHANG*
CARNEGIE MELLON UNIVERSITY, JUNIOR

SCIENCE EXPERIMENT?

In my fraternity house, we had a very old iron stove in the kitchen, which was original to the house. The stove was huge, and completely useless—it hadn't worked in decades. But nobody could move it because it was so heavy, and no trash disposal company or dumping ground would accept it—not even if we paid them to take it! It seemed as though our house was stuck with this old relic for another 80 years.

Then one night we had a brainstorm. In the middle of the night, about 10 of us hoisted this piece of useless iron onto a dolly, and rolled it across campus to the Science Center. Now, in the lobby of the college's Science Center was a small museum of scientific artifacts (you know, like a 200 year-old microscope, or a skeleton of a 1 million-year old small rodent). So, we found a nice little nook for the stove (right in between some nice relics) and placed a professional looking sign on the stove which said: "Random Kinetic Energy Enhancer, circa 1842." Only a science geek would know that that is another way of saying: "This is an old stove."

The relic stayed for about a week, then was hauled off by the University. We didn't pay a dime.

—I.L.S.
WESLEYAN UNIVERSITY, 1987

THE CAT IN THE FRAT?

Dr. Seuss (Theodore Geisel, class of 1925) studied at Dartmouth. Internet legend has it that he decorated his fraternity house walls with drawings of his strange characters; we're not sure it's a true story, but who cares?

⭐ **IF YOU'RE GOING TO JOIN A SORORITY,** bail after the first year—two years at most. The whole sorority-fraternity thing inhibits having a rich and diverse college experience. You're lumped together with a small percentage of the campus population, and you cheat yourself of the opportunity to meet interesting people who wouldn't be caught dead on Greek Row. At first, a sorority or fraternity can be comforting. You just left home for the first time, and being around people who are like you can put you at ease; that's OK. But after the first year or two, it's not doing you any favors. Get out. Find the best in the bunch, keep them as friends, then bail. You may catch flak, and you won't be a lifetime member of your frat or sorority. But you will be better off, finding your own way on your own terms.

—*B.P.*
FLORIDA STATE UNIVERSITY, 1991

• • • • • • • •

WHILE I DIDN'T JOIN A FRATERNITY, I did decide to join an engineering society at my school. This one was pretty hell-bent on getting drunk every weekend, like most fraternities at my school. This naturally became my attitude in my freshman year, and even continued into my second year. Try to keep school your priority during the week (as much as possible) so that your weekend social life doesn't intrude on your studies, when drinking affects grades. Also, ask yourself if it's worth $1000 a semester to be in one of these groups. (Mine was only about $160 a year, which was very appealing.) You'll probably also come to a point when you're a senior and you realize that these groups aren't as exciting as they were when you were a freshman.

—*ANONYMOUS*
UNIVERSITY OF VIRGINIA, SENIOR

AFTER A WHILE, YOU GET KIND OF BORED with college, and it's good to meet people and network through fraternities. I've met a lot of people from different walks of life. I've learned a lot about people. There were some people that I met while pledging, and I had a feeling I might not like them. But then I got to know them and I ended up liking them.

You shouldn't rush frats the first semester. Get acquainted with the university. The second semester, it's a good thing to do. It's something to complement your academics. It helps keep you focused.

—*RON SILVER*
UNIVERSITY OF MARYLAND, JUNIOR

• • • • • • • •

"I pledged a fraternity and it gave me a way to meet people. It really helped out. If you use it as a tool, you can meet people and down the road, it can get you jobs. When you first start out, it gets you into the social events and you make friends with a lot of people."

—*JOSH HERN*
PURDUE UNIVERSITY, 1998

BEFORE COLLEGE, I WAS VERY ANTI-SORORITY; I thought they were evil. But now, even though I'm not in a sorority, I live with sorority girls, and they're all my good friends. I go to lots of their functions and have a great time. It's not a big deal if you're not in a sorority. It's only a big deal the first few weeks of the year and then the five days of Rush. During Rush I just remind myself that I do have friends; they're just all busy this week. If you're not sure whether you want to join a fraternity or sorority, remember that you can still join and it doesn't have to be the top priority in your life. Join; just don't become president. Sororities and fraternities are a great way to make a big school seem smaller.

—*SUMMER J.*
UNIVERSITY OF VIRGINIA, SENIOR

• • • • • • • •

"I avoided frat parties until I was a senior. That's when I knew better."

—*ANONYMOUS*
UNIVERSITY OF RHODE ISLAND, SOPHOMORE

• • • • • • • •

I PLEDGED A SORORITY and dropped out the first semester. I didn't like the social aspect of it. It was like high school, and I was trying to get away from that. They judge you on appearances. It wasn't rude, but I didn't like it. I like being more independent.

—*ALYSSA*
JAMES MADISON UNIVERSITY, SOPHOMORE

I RUSHED THAT WINTER out of boredom and mild curiosity. If you like sororities, that's great. I remember being at one house with another theater major and we thought the women there were just silly. So this girl and I purposefully started acting ridiculous and saying all this outrageous and obnoxious stuff to get ourselves "cut" from the house, as a sort of experiment. The next day, that house didn't cut us; we couldn't believe it.

—*ANONYMOUS*

• • • • • • • •

JOIN A FRATERNITY OR SORORITY. Realize what you like and don't like. I joined a frat, and my first year it was a lot of fun and very helpful. It provided me with social outlets and allowed me to get exposed to the university. If you don't do that, you're potentially limiting your experiences. But after two years I realized the fallacy of the whole fraternity system. It's myopic and close-minded. You're dealing with very homogeneous people, so in the long run, you're probably limiting your experience. But if you recognize that, you're ahead of the game.

—*W.J.F.*
GEORGETOWN UNIVERSITY, JUNIOR

• • • • • • • •

BIG FRATERNITY/ SORORITY SCHOOLS

• Washington and Lee University (Virginia)

• Depauw University (Indiana)

• University of Indiana–Bloomington

• University of Colorado–Boulder

• Birmingham-Southern College (Alabama)

THE FIRST FEW PARTIES OF THE YEAR, they'll let pretty much anyone in just to get themselves known for killer parties. After a few weeks, though, they start patrolling their parties by placing a few brothers in the driveway to tell the masses that "the house occupancy is full, but try back later." If you drop the name of a brother, though, they'll let you in. So at the first party of the year, I randomly met a guy named Steve and found out he was from Louisiana. So every time I went back, I told the guys in the driveway I knew "Steve from Louisiana," and it worked like a charm. I passed Steve from Louisiana's name on to whoever wanted to hang out at that frat.

—ASHLEY LEAVELL
BOSTON UNIVERSITY, SENIOR

• • • • • • • •

Imagine it is just some elaborate *Saturday Night Live* skit in which you are grudgingly playing along.

—ANONYMOUS

DO NOT BELIEVE THE HYPE that Greek organizations feed you during your first semester in college. You will not find friends who will be there for you if you join a fraternity or sorority just as you get into college. These organizations try get freshmen to join by saying that this is the best way to find friends. On the contrary, it is the best way to exclude yourself from people who can become your best friends, and to get a narrow view of college life. Before joining a Greek organization, find an organization that shares your interests, perhaps something where you can have a wide variety of friends.

—D.
MOREHEAD STATE, JUNIOR

More Wisdom: Good Stuff that Doesn't Fit Anywhere Else

Had just about enough advice by now? But wait, there's more! Though they don't fit in tidy categories, these thoughts are just as important. Take them with you, and enjoy!

ANYTHING RANDOM IS BAD. Don't allow them to pick a random roommate for you; find one and request him. Don't go into a random dorm or room; pick your own. Same thing with the meal plan; do your due diligence and find out what the options are or you will be unhappy with the choices made for you. This is true for life as well as college. Don't be a sheep: Take charge.

—*ANGEL NYA*
CARNEGIE MELLON UNIVERSITY, SOPHOMORE

DON'T TAKE YOURSELF SO SERIOUSLY. ENJOY THIS UNIQUE TIME IN YOUR LIFE.

—*TREVOR*
AMHERST COLLEGE
1957

Everyone searches for an identity their freshman year; that's one of your biggest struggles.

—*RYAN A. BROWN*
UNIVERSITY OF
NORTH CAROLINA
AT CHAPEL HILL
1998

MY FIRST DAY OF CLASS, a department chair said something that stuck with me. He said, "It's possible to go through four years of college unscathed by education. It's a tragedy if that happens." He went on to say that college is about challenging all of your preconceived notions; from your personal values to your religious values to your social values to your political values. If you have a real college experience, it should all be challenged. If you don't have the courage to face that, you're not getting as much out of college as you could. Be prepared to be challenged.

—*MICHAEL A. FEKULA*
UNIVERSITY OF MARYLAND, 1985

• • • • • • • •

IT'S HARD TO REMEMBER back to freshman year. There's a lesson there: It will pass, good and bad.

—*LINDSEY SHULTZ*
CARNEGIE MELLON UNIVERSITY, SENIOR

• • • • • • • •

IF YOU'RE NOT CAREFUL, the first year of college will be the most unhealthy year of your entire life. The food is bad for you, you're probably not exercising as much as you were in high school, you drink tons of caffeine and even more alcohol, and you don't sleep. Freshman year, try to remember to sleep more and exercise more. That way you'll be a fully functioning human being. Sometimes it's hard to pass up parties, but remember that there will be other nights and other funny stories. Choose your night.

—*SUMMER J.*
UNIVERSITY OF VIRGINIA, SENIOR

• • • • • • • •

FIND A GROUP ON CAMPUS that interests you, so you don't feel that the school is so huge.

—*STEPHANIE*
UNIVERSITY OF PENNSYLVANIA, SENIOR

✓ **KNOW WHAT YOU WANT TO DO** when you go to college. I didn't know and I didn't care. I didn't go to many classes; I just spent my time meeting people and going to parties. I did everything you weren't supposed to do: I signed up for hard classes, I didn't go to them, and I went out every night. When I was 18, I acted a lot younger.

—*A.G.S.*
UNIVERSITY OF TENNESSEE, DID NOT GRADUATE

· · · · · · · ·

" Have an open mind and try to see everything. Not everything will be your thing, but there is something that you'll find. "

—*ANONYMOUS*
UNIVERSITY OF PENNSYLVANIA, FRESHMAN

· · · · · · · ·

I WAS NEVER A FRESHMAN. When asked, I was an "undergrad," or for those not into the whole brevity thing, I was "finishing up my lower-division classes," or "in my second semester." Did this help me? Yes and no. If you are around other freshmen, you don't really have to do it; they don't need to be impressed. It works fairly well on upper-division students, though. If you tell one of them that you are a freshman, they immediately sort of shy away from you. So, use euphemisms, but use discretion, too.

—*KARLA SAIA*
SAN DIEGO STATE UNIVERSITY, JUNIOR

☆

Don't set your mind on anything the first year. Explore. That's what it's about.

—*M.M.*
NEW YORK UNIVERSITY, SENIOR

STUDENT TEACHERS

Here's the best piece of advice I think I got in four years: At the end of my freshman year, I set up a meeting with a professor who had befriended me. I had been considering taking more classes over the summer to get ahead towards my degree (yes, I was a little nerd) and so I asked, "Is the quality of the courses the same as during the year? Do the same professors teach during the summer?" He said, "The professors are the same, but the courses are not as good." He paused for a second to enjoy the look of confusion on my face. "It's the students that are generally worse. During the summer, there are a lot of high school students, trying to put something on their resume. You learn from your peers more than from the professor, you know."

My professor's advice was excellent—the people I met at college were so exceptional and taught me so much, everything from literature to physics.

—NOAH HELMAN
HARVARD UNIVERSITY, 1998

MAKE SURE YOU RESEARCH THE SCHOOL to see if everyone goes home on weekends. I attended a commuter college. Almost all the kids who live there go home over the weekends, so there's absolutely nothing to do. It would be a good idea to talk to current students about what goes on when classes aren't in session. This is even more important if you go to a school where none of your friends are going. If all the kids go home and you go there to get away from home, you have absolutely nothing to do on weekends.

—MATTHEW MOLNAR
QUEENS COLLEGE, JUNIOR

• • • • • • • •

IF YOU DON'T HAVE AN OPENNESS to the situation, you're going to have trouble. You're going to meet people of different backgrounds and beliefs, some people that have been coddled and some people that haven't. You need an openness to learn and an openness to accept. If you don't have that, you won't do very well. If you do, your experience will be a lot better.

—ZACH FRIEND
UNIVERSITY OF CALIFORNIA AT SANTA CRUZ, 2001

• • • • • • • •

MY FRESHMAN YEAR WAS GOOD, BAD, everything you could possibly imagine. The bad parts were adjusting, then readjusting, then readjusting again to leaving home and being on your own and making your life work. There was a lot to be exposed to really fast.

—J.P.G.
UNIVERSITY OF PENNSYLVANIA, SOPHOMORE

• • • • • • • •

FRESHMAN YEAR WAS NOT an endurance test—it was a friggin' celebration!

—L.
DUKE UNIVERSITY, 1985

All the trouble I got into, all the bad things that came from college, came from the social gatherings. All the good things came from people I met in the classrooms.

—J.H.
WIDENER UNIVERSITY, 1997

Never be lazy. College only happens once and it's not long enough, so take advantage of it.

—*KERRY*
GEORGETOWN UNIVERSITY, 2002

⭐ **FORM HABITS THAT WILL TRANSLATE** into career traits after your schooling is complete. This does not have to be stressful. It can be simplified:

1) Find a place that's just yours where you can study comfortably.

2) Get up early a few days a week and walk, jog, or practice something physical.

3) Do something at least one day a week that's for someone else—visit a facility where you can volunteer (not with a bunch of friends; just you).

4) Write in a journal. Give yourself time to reflect and see things through someone else's eyes.

If you get into these habits, it will carry you not only through your first year, but also through your whole college career. You'll amaze yourself at how consistent you can be. And the carryover of these habits will frame your post-school life for success, no matter what you choose to do.

—*TREVOR*
AMHERST COLLEGE, 1957

❝Have your fun, but realize you're here to get an education (and, hopefully, a degree!) Make it all worthwhile— academics and social life.❞

—*KHALIL SULLIVAN*
PRINCETON UNIVERSITY, JUNIOR

I SURVIVED MY FRESHMAN YEAR

Cursed with an annoying stammer, I always scrupulously avoided doing anything at all in front of an audience. But in my first week as a freshman I was forced to come face to face with "the stammer."

In a business management course, we were asked to debate issues given to us by our lecturers. My group was given the ridiculous proposition that "welfare benefits assist unemployment" and told to argue against it. Maintaining my treasured high-school stance of protected anonymity, I offered a few ideas to my group while steadfastly refusing to be the spokesperson for the group.

However, our dear teachers were not to be fobbed off with such an approach. They started firing questions at *all* the participants.

I waited for my turn to come. When it did, I opened my mouth to answer and . . . nothing. Zilch. I writhed and wriggled, and still nothing.

I prayed hard that the earth would open and swallow me up. I knew that I'd blown it for the rest of my college life, and all in the first week.

And then, suddenly, it came: "This form of intolerance and preconceived notions is the same that the proposers of this motion are suggesting for the unemployed."

There was total silence, then applause. I had bowled them over with an outrageous display of demagoguery. Within the month, I was a candidate for the Student Representative Council. Within the year, I was conducting workshops and making speeches before thousands. Lots of screaming, plenty of demagoguery and no end of guilt-tripping. A political career was born; I had survived my freshman year.

—PHIL CARMEL
UNIVERSITY COLLEGE–SALFORD (ENGLAND), 1985

SLEEP EARLY AND OFTEN—don't stay up till 2 a.m. because you'll never get up for your 8 a.m. class.

EAT EARLY AND OFTEN—don't skip breakfast, and eat three meals a day.

DRINK—but not too early and not too often.

—C.B., 1993

WHAT I NEGLECTED MY FRESHMAN YEAR was taking advice from professors. In high school, I always felt like my teachers didn't know what they were talking about. But the professors really do know what they're talking about, and not just in their fields. When they give you advice, listen to it. I didn't take the advice of people who could've helped me. Most freshmen have this attitude: "I got to college, so why do I need you now?" Your pride and self-confidence get in the way of re-evaluating the situation you're in. That's what it comes down to. You've got to shed your attitude; it really gets in the way.

—ZAK AMCHISLAVSKY
GEORGETOWN UNIVERSITY, SENIOR

• • • • • • • •

I WAS EXPOSED TO A LOT OF THE SCARY SIDES of people that I hadn't come so close to before. Like the time some guys beat up and killed a raccoon outside my dorm. Or the time a dormmate expressed to me that she often felt like committing suicide, and I felt like there was nothing I could do to help her, except let her know that a lot of people around her really cared about her.

—K. HARMA
WESTERN WASHINGTON UNIVERSITY, 2001

• • • • • • • •

I WAS AFRAID TO bring my collection of CDs to college; I was afraid that people would laugh at me. I thought you needed to listen to certain kinds of music once you got to college or people would make fun of you. But once I got here, I realized that wasn't the case. People listen to all different kinds of music and you can listen to whatever you want to listen to.

—BRANDON HOGAN
HOWARD UNIVERSITY, SENIOR

DON'T TALK BAD ABOUT ANYONE. My dad told me that when I was in high school and I stuck with it. No one has a bad thing to say about you if you don't say bad things about them. If they do, you realize they're not worth your time.

—*CASEY*
GEORGETOWN UNIVERSITY, SENIOR

• • • • • • • •

❝I recommend taking a year off before starting college. It gives a fantastic perspective on why you need to be sitting in classes day after day. The hard thing about it is meeting other people who have been through the same experience.❞

—*LEAH PRICE*
GEORGETOWN UNIVERSITY, SOPHOMORE

• • • • • • • •

I'M NOT NORMALLY an advice-giving person. I don't buy giving advice; who am I to tell you how to live your freshman year? Part of being a freshman is about being away from parents and doing stupid things. Doing stupid things is the best way to learn. People learn more from their own advice than anyone else's. Plus, anything you learn from is not stupid.

—*CAITLIN BERBERICH*
UNIVERSITY OF GEORGIA, 2001

Everyone searches for an identity their freshman year; that's one of your biggest struggles.

—*RYAN A. BROWN*
*UNIVERSITY OF
NORTH CAROLINA
AT CHAPEL HILL
1998*

IF YOU GO TO SCHOOL IN A BIG CITY, you have to be more careful. Watch out for your surroundings. If you have to take a route where you might have trouble, stay away from it. Take the long way. There's nothing more important than your life.

—B.L.
JOHN JAY COLLEGE OF CRIMINAL JUSTICE, GRADUATE

· · · · · · · ·

"Make a plan. Write out everything you have to do, every day. Follow that plan and stick with it. Don't let anything get in the way of taking care of that plan. It's like a schedule. Write down everything that you have to do, and get it done. Social things, everything."

—BRIAN
JAMES MADISON UNIVERSITY, JUNIOR

· · · · · · · ·

THIS IS WHAT THE REAL WORLD IS LIKE. College is diverse. Be open to new experiences. Don't judge people on whether or not they get wasted on the weekends. That's just one aspect of a person.

—ERIC MCINTOSH
UNIVERSITY OF NORTH CAROLINA AT CHAPEL HILL, JUNIOR

I'M FROM NEW YORK and I went to a very rural, small, homogeneous, southern school my freshman year. It was a bit of a culture shock. I was in classes with white, upper-middle-class kids and that was it. On your tour they say it's diverse, but I don't know what their definition of that is; it's not the New York definition. I didn't realize how much it would affect me, not having access to plays and restaurants and jazz clubs. You had to really travel if you wanted to do anything that would stimulate you. I knew by November that it was not where I wanted to spend my college life. People make you think your decision to pick a college is the end-all of your entire life. So find a place that looks interesting, and figure out what's important to you before you check out a college. Don't be influenced by a beautiful campus or the nice people in your tour. Expect that you're going to spend four years there, but know that if you don't, it's not jail; you can transfer. College is about *you*, not the school.

—HANNAH SMITH
HARVARD UNIVERSITY, JUNIOR

CAN YOU SPELL "WHITE HOUSE"?

Some U.S. Presidents who never went to college:

George Washington
Andrew Jackson
Abraham Lincoln
Andrew Johnson
Harry Truman

" You can graduate with decent grades, you can do nothing and just get four years older, or you can suck the marrow out of your university and garner all the knowledge, academic and other, that comes your way. The choice and your future are in your hands. Don't go to college and just get four years older. **"**

—*Adam*
Elon University, Sophomore

• • • • • • • •

Remember, everyone else is in the same boat as you. College is your first taste of freedom, but it comes with a lot of responsibility. No freshman has it all figured out, so if you find people that act like they do, they're drunk or lying.

—*Anonymous*
Union College

• • • • • • • •

Use your Exxon gas card to buy cases of beer and snacks, because gas stations don't card.

—*Matt Field*
Syracuse University, 1993

☆ **COLLEGE IS A VERY BIG TRANSITION** from high school. I went to boarding school for five years and therefore felt that I'd be able to make the transition fairly easily. In boarding school you live away from home and you deal with stuff on your own; the independence thing. But I was at a school where the teacher had a class of twenty, he knew every single one of us, and helped us out. Teachers would notice if there was a problem. In college you're basically left to work by yourself and sort everything out by yourself. If you haven't quite figured it out and it shows in your grades or in what teachers say of you, then at the end of the day you're just in the doghouse—there's really no one to help you, unless you actively go and ask for help.

—*IAN MOK*
HARVARD UNIVERSITY, SOPHOMORE

COLLEGE FOOTBALL'S CONTRIBUTIONS TO MANKIND

1. Gatorade was named for the University of Florida (football) Gators, where it was developed in 1965. Coach Ray Graves's Florida team—powered by the potion concocted by a UF med-school professor—came from behind to defeat heavily favored Louisiana State in 102-degree heat, and a legend was born.

2. The football huddle originated at Gallaudet University, a liberal-arts college for the deaf, when the football team found that opposing teams were reading their signed messages and intercepting plays.

THE BEST YEAR OF YOUR LIFE

The experience of leaving my freshman year of college is among the most memorable times of my life, along with graduating from high school. Coming to college, I was scared shitless and had no idea how I was going to survive. In May, the heat hit me hard as I was packing up my life into a few duffle bags and sweeping out the room that witnessed my first attempts at independence. I peeled off the walls the pictures of people I once saw

every day and swore always to be best friends with, who became people I only talked to once in a while on IM. It sounds sad, but my high-school friends and I had gone our separate ways and discovered new lives with people we once called strangers. With these strangers I now had inside jokes, crazy blurry memories, and new pictures to plaster

on my wall. Not to say that college is always amazing: the food sucks, your roommate will smell, your professor can be an asshole, there are morning classes, and the guy you can't believe you hooked up with will live down the hall all semester long. It's what makes college college. With all the bad, there is the good. With all your worries and all your fears, freshman year won't suck that bad—it might even be the best year of your life.

—KAREN
STATE UNIVERSITY OF NEW YORK AT NEW PALTZ, SOPHOMORE

CREDITS

P. 27: *The Insider's Guide to the Colleges 2004*. Copyright © 2004 Yale Daily News Publishing Company, Inc. All rights reserved. Reprinted with permission.

P. 35: *The College Board Handbook 2004*. Copyright © 2003 by College Board. All rights reserved. Reproduced with permission. www.collegeboard.com.

P. 42: The Princeton Review, www.princetonreview.com.

P. 43: The Princeton Review; www.princetonreview.com.

P. 89: College Board press release, August 26, 2003, www.collegeboard.com.

P. 94: The New York Times, September 3, 2003.

P. 97: www.whitehouse.gov/news/releases/2001/05/20010521_2.html

P. 106: www.oznet.ksu.edu/dp_grsi/about.htm

P. 120: Hobson's College View Survey; www.collegeview.com.

P. 130: *The Insider's Guide to the Colleges, 2004*. Copyright © 2004 Yale Daily News Publishing Company, Inc. All rights reserved. Reprinted with permission.

P. 142: *The College Board College Handbook 2004*. Copyright © 2003 by College Board. All rights reserved. Reproduced with permission. www.collegeboard.com.

P. 148: The Princeton Review; www.princetonreview.com.

P. 154: *The College Board College Handbook 2004*. Copyright © 2003 by College Board. All rights reserved. Reproduced with permission. www.collegeboard.com.

P. 190: *The Insider's Guide to the Colleges, 2004*. Copyright © 2004 Yale Daily News Publishing Company, Inc. All rights reserved. Reprinted with permission.

P. 191: *The Insider's Guide to the Colleges, 2004*. Copyright © 2004 Yale Daily News Publishing Company, Inc. All rights reserved. Reprinted with permission.

P. 211: The Princeton Review; www.princetonreview.com.

P. 212: www.hsph.harvard.edu/cas/Documents/trends-pressRelease

P. 214: *The College Board College Handbook 2004*. Copyright © 2003 by College Board. All rights reserved. Reproduced with permission. www.collegeboard.com.

P. 220: www.bitoffun.com/Funfacts.com

P. 235: www.trumanlibrary.org

P. 237: www.pr.gallaudet.edu; www.rgp.ufl.edu/explore/v08n1/gatorade.html

ADVICE FROM:

American Repertory Theater at Harvard
American University
Amherst College
Auburn University
Barnard College
Boston College
Boston University
Bowling Green State University
Brown University
Bryn Mawr College
Cal Poly San Luis Obispo
Calvin College
Carnegie Mellon University
Clemson University
College of San Mateo
Columbia University
Cornell University
Curtis Institute of Music
DeSales University
Diablo Valley College
Dominican University
Duke University
Elon University
Emory University
Florida A&M University
Florida State University
Foothill College
Frostburg State University
George Washington University
Georgetown University
Georgia Southern University
Georgia State University
Georgia Institute of Technology
Hamilton College
Harvard University
Howard University
Hunter College
Indiana University
James Madison University
John Jay College of Criminal Justice
Johns Hopkins University
Kingsborough Community College
Louisiana State University
Massachusetts Institute of Technology
Miami University
Michigan Technological University
Mississippi State University
Moorhead State University
Morehead State University
New York University
Northwestern University
Oberlin University
Oxford College
Penn State University
Princeton University
Purdue University
Queens College
Rhodes College
Rutgers University
St. Lawrence University

San Diego State University
San Francisco State University
San Jose State University
Santa Barbara City College
Santa Clara University
Sonoma State University
Spring Hill College
Stanford University
State University of New York at Albany
State University of New York at Binghamton
State University of New York at New Paltz
Syracuse University
Trinity University
United States Military Academy at West Point
Union College
University College–Salford (England)
University of California at Berkeley
University of California at Davis
University of California at Irvine
University of California at Santa Barbara
University of California at Santa Cruz
University of Chicago
University of Colorado
University of Connecticut
University of Delaware
University of Florida
University of Georgia
University of Illinois
University of Maryland
University of Maryland–College Park
University of Maryland–Baltimore County
University of Massachusetts
University of Massachusetts at Amherst
University of Michigan
University of Missouri
University of New Hampshire
University of North Carolina
University of North Carolina at Chapel Hill
University of Notre Dame
University of Oregon
University of Pennsylvania
University of Rhode Island
University of Rochester
University of South Florida
University of Tennessee
University of Tennessee at Martin
University of Texas
University of Texas at Austin
University of Virginia
University of Wisconsin–Stevens Point
Villanova
Wake Forest
Wellesley College
Wesleyan University
Westfield State College
Western Washington University
Widener University
Williams College
Yale University

HELP YOUR FRIENDS SURVIVE!

Order extra copies of How to Survive Your Freshman Year.

Check your local bookstore or order here

Please send me _____ copies of How to Survive Your Freshman Year.

Enclose $12.95 for each copy. Include $4 for shipping and handling for one book, and $2 for each additional book. Georgia residents must include applicable sales tax. Payment must accompany orders. Please allow 3 weeks for delivery.

My check for $_____ is enclosed.
Please charge my __ Visa __ MasterCard __ American Express

Name _____

Organization _____

Address _____

City/State/Zip _____

Phone _____Email _____

Credit card # _____

Exp. Date _____Signature _____

Make checks payable to HUNDREDS OF HEADS BOOKS and mail to:

Hundreds of Heads Books, Inc.
2221 Peachtree Road
Suite D-230
Atlanta, Georgia 30309

Fax : 212-937-2220
www.howisurvived.com

Mail to:

HUNDREDS OF HEADS BOOKS, INC.
2221 Peachtree Road
Suite D-230
Atlanta, Georgia 30309

And be sure to visit www.howisurvived.com

LET'S PUT OUR HEADS TOGETHER! TELL US YOUR STORY!

Put yourself in our next book—share your wisdom and experiences with other HUNDREDS OF HEADS readers. Use the form on the reverse side, or visit www.howisurvived.com.

Here's my story/advice on surviving

❏ **FRESHMAN YEAR** (your college and year of graduation:_____)

❏ **DATING** (how many years have you been dating: _____)

❏ **MARRIAGE** (how many years have you been married: _____)

❏ **A BABY** (ages and sexes of your children – e.g. boy 4, girl 2:_____)

❏ **IN-LAWS** (how many years have you had in-laws:_____)

❏ **A TEENAGER** (ages and sexes of your children – e.g. girl 19, boy 17:_____)

❏ **A JOB** (how many years have you been working:_____

   profession/job:_____)

❏ _____ **OTHER TOPIC** (you pick)

Name _____

(Optional) ❏ Use my initials only   ❏ Anonymous

City/State: _____

(Note: Your entry in the book will also include city/state and the descriptive information above.)

How should we contact you:

email: _____   other: _____

Waiver: All entries are property of Hundreds of Heads Books, Inc., and may be edited, published in any medium, etc. By submitting content, you grant Hundreds of Heads Books, Inc. and its affiliates a royalty-free, perpetual, irrevocable, non-exclusive right (including any moral rights) and license to use, reproduce, modify, adapt, publish, translate, create derivative works from, distribute, communicate to the public, perform and display the content (in whole or in part) worldwide and/or to incorporate it in other works in any form, media, or technology now known or later developed, for the full term of any Rights that may exist in such content, and to identify you (with the information above) as the contributor of content you submit.

Here's my story/advice:

_____

_____

_____

_____

_____

_____

_____

_____

_____

_____

_____

_____

_____

_____

_____

_____

_____

_____

_____

_____

_____

_____

_____

_____

_____

_____

Mail to:

HUNDREDS OF HEADS BOOKS, INC.
2221 Peachtree Road
Suite D-230
Atlanta, Georgia 30309